The Contagion of Matter

*Nearsights: Selected Poems
of Valerio Magrelli*

*Instructions on How to Read a
Newspaper and Other Poems*

VANISHING POINTS

VALERIO

MAGRELLI

VANISHING

POINTS

POEMS TRANSLATED

FROM THE ITALIAN BY

JAMIE McKENDRICK

FARRAR STRAUS GIROUX

NEW YORK

FARRAR STRAUS GIROUX

18 West 18th Street, New York 10011

Copyright © 2010 by Valerio Magrelli
Translation copyright © 2010 by Jamie McKendrick
All rights reserved
Printed in the United States of America
Originally published (without the Italian text) in 2010 by Faber
    and Faber Limited, Great Britain, as *The Embrace: Selected Poems*
Bilingual edition published in the United States by Farrar, Straus and Giroux
First edition, 2010

Library of Congress Cataloging-in-Publication Data
Magrelli, Valerio, 1957–
    [Selections. English & Italian. 2010]
    Vanishing points : poems / Valerio Magrelli;
    translated by Jamie McKendrick. — 1st. ed.
        p. cm.
    English and Italian.
    Originally published: Great Britain : Faber and Faber,
    as The embrace: selected poems. 2010.
    ISBN: 978-0-374-28253-0
        1. Magrelli, Valerio, 1957—Translations into English.
    I. McKendrick, Jamie, 1955– II. Title.

PQ4873.A3624A26 2010
851'.914—dc22
                                                        2009045652

Designed and composed by Quemadura

www.fsgbooks.com

10 9 8 7 6 5 4 3 2 1

CONTENTS

Prosegue il catalogo delle vegetazioni — "The catalogue of vegetation continues"—begins one early poem by Valerio Magrelli. Only some lines later do we realize that the Linnaean impulse behind the poem has thought itself, its own thinking, rather than botany as its subject, but we already sense how the scene of possibly thankless, methodical labor is a wry image for the book he is writing:

> Like a canvas,
> much overpainted,
> on which many different
> hands have worked . . .

Before its end, this characteristically brief, untitled poem has set in play a series of oppositions: scientific/artistic, solitary/collaborative, internal/external.

Magrelli's remarkable first book, published in 1980 when he was twenty-three, bears the somewhat forbidding title *Ora serrata retinae*, which would seem more in the way of an oculist's textbook than a collection of poems. The term signifies the jagged edge, specifically "the irregular anterior margin of the *pars optica* of the retina." Each poem in the book is an instrument of perception, with a clear circumference and a scrupulously observed area of concern. They highlight a particular small feature of an internal, often nocturnal landscape and yet cumulatively they bring a haunting and abundant panorama into view. A demonstrative quality is to the fore—and it's significant that as many as thirteen poems in the book have a "questo" or "questa" ("this") in the first line. The poems examine the "I" as well as the eye

that examines. Rhetorically, they also reconfigure the infolding move-
ment: "I think of the tailor / who uses himself for a roll of cloth." They
proceed painstakingly with their "catalogue of vegetation," describing
the moods and torsions of perceiving. Only when they, the poems,
have acquired sufficient surety of their own visual and conceptual bias
do they gradually and inexorably move outward.

The book was greeted with quite unprecedented acclaim by many
of Italy's most significant writers and received praise from poets as far
afield as Octavio Paz and Joseph Brodsky. Not since Eugenio Mon-
tale's *Ossi di seppia* has there been such a consensus that here, at last,
was a voice inhabited by the whole language and culture, shaping it to
its own purposes. Reading them again, a quarter of a century after
their publication, what's striking is the sheer nerve of the enterprise:
poems scribbled down like diary jottings in a notebook with what looks
like a radical economy of means, often a single galvanizing metaphor,
that focus so resolutely on an aspect of consciousness. The tone is dry
and scientific, almost forensic, seemingly hostile to any lyrical effects,
and yet again and again, almost despite itself, a fierce concentration
propels the poems out beyond the familiar. Elizabeth Bishop's often
quoted letter on Darwin, which praises his outwardly directed "self-
forgetful, perfectly useless concentration," "sees the lonely young
man, his eyes fixed on facts and minute details, sinking or sliding gid-
dily off into the unknown." Something analogous occurs in these po-
ems with a procedure that is precisely contrary.

The compressed, punning title *Nature e venature* (Natures and
Veinings, 1987) of Magrelli's second volume retains an element of the
physiological but places it in a wider landscape. Little could seem fur-
ther from traditional nature poetry than these curt meditations, and
yet they share with a poet like Hopkins an extraordinary impulse not

merely to describe but to encompass, almost themselves to perform, the underlying principles of growth and form. Hopkins would be at home within this precisely observed, recursive and inscaped world of veinings, cloud formations, Fibonacci numbers. Unlike Hopkins, though, with his flaming palette of "gold-vermillion" and "skies of couple-colour as a brinded cow," Magrelli's poems have the subdued tones of Analytical Cubism or verge on monochrome like Morandi: it's more often as though the world is seen by X-ray or lamplight or moonlight. Even the moonlight has artificial traits, as in his poem "The moonlight is a work of art . . ."—his coolly irreverent take on an outworn topos.

His third collection is *Esercizi di tiptologia* (Typtological Exercises, 1992). The word "typtology" comes from the Greek *typtein*, to beat or batter, and refers to the table-rapping in spiritualist séances and, in Italian, to the language of tapping which prisoners use to communicate. The title marks a shift from the first volume's concern with the visual to acoustic phenomena and, by extension, to language itself. "Exercises" has a musical provenance and is far from the kind of communication we might expect of wall-tapping. The head-on collision in the title between leisure and urgency, between contemplation and need, is a paradox to which the poems themselves bear witness.

All this would seem to make of Magrelli a scholarly, philosophical, cerebral poet. And yet the astonishing immediacy of the images and the precision of the language carry an emotional charge. A love poem such as "The Embrace," from his third book, excavates beneath the domestic, and by way of the central heating is led to the prospect of millennial destruction on which the frail moment of affection is based. The two flames recall the eerie double flame of Ulysses and Diomedes in Canto XXV of Dante's *Inferno*. This is one example of the way Magrelli's poems quietly situate themselves at the center of a tradition that they question and qualify. His poems describe the process of their composition, and their language keeps measuring its own capacity to observe the world.

Another example can be found in his poem "Rosebud," whose first line in Italian, "Non pretendo di dire la parola" (I do not claim to speak the word) can't fail for an Italian reader to evoke the first line of Montale's famous poem "Non chiederci la parola che squadra da ogni lato/l'anima nostra informe . . ." (Don't ask from us the word that squares off on every side / our formless soul . . .). It has the typically Montalian, negative incipit and the feel of a manifesto poem, concerned with a possible, and possibly threatened, language. The title alludes to Orson Welles's *Citizen Kane*: "Rosebud" is what Kane called his childhood sled but is also a sly reference to the name that the newspaper magnate William Randolph Hearst gave to his mistress's vagina. With its sense of the evasiveness of language and its own peculiar, witty self-referentiality the poem moves a fair distance beyond its forebear.

If the technology of the first book was utterly basic—a pencil and a notebook, the present moment of introspection—the third book is populated by current media, the telescreen, for example, and the fourth, *Didascalie per la lettura di un giornale*, by the image and sections of a newspaper. *Instructions for Reading a Newspaper* is a long poem in which each of the shorter poems corresponds to a section of the newspaper, such as Games, Horoscopes, Obituaries, and so on. The poem "Readers' Letters" is a canny device for allowing entrance to the more personal and lyrical, otherwise excluded. Even the book's title suggests a kind of antipoetry. The decision for poetry to found itself on the throwaway, the quotidian, the mechanically reproduced, recalls Joyce setting part of his epic *Ulysses* in a newspaper office— with an added, disturbing, almost elegiac touch now that newspapers are no longer our dominant mode of purveying information and news. The poem anatomizes an institution, its economics, its way of reproducing reality, and subjects the familiar to an estranging scrutiny. Walter Benjamin's argument that the organization of newspapers has a way of fragmenting our knowledge of the world is very apt here:

> Man's inner concerns do not have their issueless private character by nature. They do so only when he is increasingly unable to assimilate the data of the world around him by way of experience. Newspapers constitute one of many evidences of such an inability. If it were the intention of the press to have the reader assimilate the information as part of his own experience, it would not achieve its purpose. But its intention is just the opposite, and it is achieved: to isolate what happens from the realm in which it could affect the reader. The principles of journalistic information (freshness of the news, brevity, comprehensibility, and, above all, lack of connection between the individual news items) contribute as much to this as does the make-up of the pages and the paper's style.*

For all their brevity and their fragmentary style, these poems, as so often in Magrelli, combat that "lack of connection" which Benjamin intuits. In mimicking a newspaper format, they work in the opposite direction and bristle with connectivity.

*From "On Some Motifs in Baudelaire," in Walter Benjamin, *Illuminations: Essays and Reflections*, translated from the German by Harry Zohn and edited by Hannah Arendt (New York: Schocken, 1968), p. 158.

The idea of fragments, paradoxically, and of anatomy unites much of Magrelli's poetry. Throughout his work there is an insistence on the corporeal. One poem from his second book describes the extraction of a wisdom tooth (in Italian, *il dente di giudizio*). It is not a simple operation: the tooth has to be worked at, broken into three parts, before it comes free. The tripartite fate of the tooth is mirrored in the three stanzaic divisions of the poem as though in homage to the kind of exact correspondence between poem and thing we encounter in Francis Ponge's work. The relief of sleep at the price of bodily integrity or of wisdom is quietly hinted at, and this kind of unconsoling awareness is often painfully evident in the poems.

But there are other threads to this eleven-line poem that give an odd sacral quality to the object as though it were both suffering the process of martyrdom and itself being turned into a holy relic. It is referred to as a sacred fish, it's *segnato*—marked out as a target but also, in the context, signed with stigmata or with the cross—as well as *segato* (*segnato* with an extracted *n*)—sawed through, as though it were a particularly luckless saint. Further seams of geological imagery and of artisan vocabulary run through the poem, and it's in this context that the slow and freighted movement, the elaboration and unraveling of his language, are utterly essential to the whole design.

As Jonathan Galassi, Montale's translator, remarked of Magrelli, "his poems are not simply self-referential, but always advance an argument with and about life." One among many examples is "The Vanishing Point," a poem that tries to imagine how it might be to write a picture, say, like Uccello's "Hunt by Night," but to inscribe it in the medium of time as opposed to space. This poem is a far cry from the run-of-the-mill picture poem and an intriguing exploration of how we perceive through language. Its vanishing point, having become a temporal rather than a spatial coordinate, lets us rethink both kinds of composition—the pictorial and poetic.

Magrelli's most recent book, *Disturbi del sistema binario* (Disruptions of the Binary System, 2006), follows and reinforces the tendency of *Instructions for Reading a Newspaper* in making a book of poems an exploration of a unitary (or, in this case, binary) theme. The concerns of the poems range from the domestic to the political, considering notions of doubleness, hybrids, and antitheses—its finale is a brilliantly inventive sequence on that visual pun the *anatra-lepre* (the duck-hare, usually known in English as the duck-rabbit), in this case a kind of zoological Jekyll and Hyde. The sequence alternates roman and italic print. The idea of doubleness—and duplicity—so thoroughly explored in this poem has been a feature of Magrelli's world from the start, and can be seen in miniature, though already fully formed, in an early poem such as "A groove / like the vertical join / in plastic figurines / cuts me in two, two sides, / two slopes . . ." or in the poem on cloning, "Health: Dolly's Eye," in his penultimate book.

For all the variety of subject and approach, for all the formidable development from volume to volume, Magrelli's poetry has always had immense cohesion. Whole books can be read as sequences, and frequently the lack of titles for individual poems emphasizes this continuity. Tadeusz Różewicz, a poet with whom Magrelli has more in common than he has with most of his Italian contemporaries, speaks of his own "dogged revision, repetition, returning to the same material and so . . . to the end" as "the most valuable element" in all his work. In neither poet does this imply a narrowness, but rather a necessary depth and force. I can think of few living poets who have evolved a style so equal to and so inclusive of the most resistant aspects of modernity. A Magrelli poem is equipped to address and carry something back from subjects as various as hijackings, radioactive contamination, dinosaur toys, sheep cloning, recycling, graffiti, skateboarding, and environmental destruction. As Marianne Moore said of her ostrich, "He 'Digesteth Harde Yron.'"

A NOTE ON THE TRANSLATION

The first poem of Magrelli's that I read, some ten years ago, was "L'abbraccio" ("The Embrace"). My immediate response was such a turbulent mixture of recognition, awe, and envy that the only way I could still the chaos was to see if I could write it in English. Besides, I was intensely curious to discover whether what I admired so much in it might survive the passage. Before this, I'd translated a few Italian poems but with little appetite and mixed results. Turning "L'abbraccio" into English, I was surprised to discover, actually felt like writing a poem, carried with it the same excitement and pleasure. It seemed to me a fluke, a one-off event, but some years later, in a slightly freer style, I translated his untitled "Amo i gesti imprecisi," which I called "The Tic." For the reader who doesn't have Italian, it's only fair to note what kind of liberties are taken. Apart from the addition of a title, there are other deviations. The sentry is given an "insubordinate eyelid," and forgets what was in the cup, where the original is starker. In the last line, "Dentro qualcosa balla," the verb *ballare*, whose usual meaning is "to dance," in the case of machinery, as here, suggests something clanking or ticking, something out of kilter. My solution, "throbs," may not add up perfectly but it picks up the "cuore," the heart, which Magrelli places midpoint in his poem, and contains a sense of longing as well as a hint of physical peril. Magrelli's poem is like a modern, wittily dysfunctional update on that Provençal tradition of the *plazer*, a poem that comprises a list of favorite things. For all the departures from the original, I feel I haven't betrayed its essential direction.

Another example that might stand for a different kind of making free is my version of "Parlano" ("They Talk") which was one of the next that I attempted. Here I have put the unrhymed poem into rhyme— a labor-intensive, counterintuitive maneuver, where more normally in translation it's the reverse that occurs. My excuse for this is that I wanted to intensify the acoustics. With so much at risk of being lost, there has to be the chance of listening out for where a translation might go in the new language, of looking out for what the new language might possibly *add*.

When I had done a dozen or so translations I began to think a whole book might be worth attempting, but it was only many years after that first encounter that I set about completing it in a less sporadic fashion. The initial feeling of excitement revived. Where earlier I'd thought of the process as a lucky, random, unrepeatable exchange, I found more and more of his poems elicited a similar engagement— not just petty theft but grand larceny. In other words, what had drawn me in the first instance to a particular poem was latent or lying in wait with the same intensity of recognition in far more poems than I'd expected.

Much theorizing about translation is, and has long been, concerned with arguments over the relative claims of domesticating or estranging strategies. Often ignored, where poetry's concerned, are the different kinds of strangeness that poetry itself brings into the equation. Far more interesting than general questions of the differences between two languages is the poem's own divergence from normal use in the original language. The translator must then come to terms with (at least) two different kinds of strangeness. It's probably easier to arrive at some untroubled and consistent-sounding theoretical approach if you know little about the language you're translating from; sadly, even an extensive knowledge guarantees practically nothing, except (only perhaps) the absence of gaffes. Aside from the genuinely bilingual and some rarely gifted linguists, however well you know another language it will always remain exterior and opaque in some respects, and poetry, in which that language is paradoxically both most at home and most idiosyncratic, will remain an even more vertiginous challenge. These spots of opacity, though, may have the effect on the foreign translator of heightening attention so that the act of reading is, in more than one sense, an act of listening out. The translator is in the first place a kind of "listener-out," and then must go on to listen in, must thoroughly absorb what's alien to make it his or her own.

Even here the same problems return. Translating could then become an act of appropriation or, worse, expropriation. Lowell's *Imitations*, which continue to exert an influence today, belong to this virtuoso tradition, although their triumphs tend to be most admired by those with little knowledge of the languages and the original poems he was "imitating." Elizabeth Bishop, who voiced serious misgivings about *Imitations*, offers an alternative in her translations of the Brazilian poets Carlos Drummond de Andrade and Vinicius de Moraes: a severe adherence to the original that doesn't sacrifice vitality and formal invention. These are just two points along an infinite succession, and they don't represent wholly opposed tendencies anyway—there is no way of miraculously ridding a translation of the translator's voice and limitations. Translators serve the original best by extending the former and coping with the latter as best they can. My own approach has been catholic, pragmatic, even opportunistic rather than consistent with any theory. I have tried to sense the possibility each poem, with its own peculiar demands, opens up within the new language. I've ditched those (a fair number at that) where I'd failed to bring anything new into the English, and any that, on checking later, seemed too close to Anthony Molino's earlier, authoritative translations.*

*Anthony Molino's translations of Magrelli's first two books, along with new translations by Riccardo Duranti and Anamaria Crowe Serrano of Magrelli's fourth book, were reprinted in *Instructions on How to Read a Newspaper and Other Poems*, edited by Anthony Molino (2009).

FROM

ORA SERRATA

RETINAE

1980

ORA SERRATA

RETINAE

1980

Non ho un bicchiere d'acqua
sopra il letto:
ho questo quaderno.
A volte ci segno parole nel buio
e il giorno che segue le trova
deformate dalla luce e mute.
Sono oggetti notturni
posati ad asciugare,
che nel sole s'incrinano
e scoppiano. Restano pezzi sparsi,
povere ceramiche del sonno
che colmano la pagina.
È il cimitero del pensiero
che si raccoglie tra le mie mani.

It's not a glass of water that I keep
beside the bed,
but this notebook.
Sometimes I sign words there in the dark
and the following day finds them
dumbstruck and battered by the light.
They're nocturnal things
left out to dry
that wrinkle and burst
in sunlight. Only scattered bits and pieces
remain, faint ceramics of sleep
that overflow the page.
It's the graveyard of the thought
that shapes itself between my hands.

Questo quaderno è il mio scudo,
trincea, periscopio, feritoia.
Guardo da una stanza buia nella luce;
non visto vedo, vergognosa scienza della spia.
Assegno che ad ogni riga cresce,
miracolo dei pani moltiplicati,
libro mastro di perdite e guadagni
nel lungo arco dei commerci umani.
Superficie di carne su cui gratto
prima di prender sonno, e che carezzo
come un piede
dopo il cammino del giorno.

This notebook serves me as a shield,
a trench, a periscope, a loophole.
I look from a dark room into the light;
unseen I see—the spy's furtive tradecraft.
I arrange it so that every line
multiplies like the miracle of the loaves
—a ledger of losses and gains
to reckon up the eras of human commerce.
Surface of flesh on which I scratch
before sleeping, which I caress and knead
like an instep
after the day's hard slog.

Un tempo si portava sulla pagina
il giorno trascorso, adesso invece
si parla solamente del parlare.
Come se nel tragitto
dall'impressione alla carta
si fosse dischiusa una vertigine.
Dunque passando
dall'una all'altra sponda
tutte le mercanzie vanno perdute
e il viaggiatore
dimenticato il viaggio
sa narrare soltanto del pericolo corso.

Once you brought to the page
the day that had passed, but now
you speak only of speech.
As if in the journey the impression
makes on its way to paper
a chasm had opened.
So moving from one
to the other shore
all the merchandise has been lost
and the traveler,
having forgotten his travels,
can only tell the dangers he's survived.

C'è un momento in cui il corpo
si raccoglie nel respiro
e il pensiero si sospende ed esita.
Anche le cose
commosse dalla luna
subiscono il sospiro delle maree
o le flessioni dolci dell'eclisse.
E il legno delle barche
si gonfia nell'acqua delicato.

There's a moment when the body
gathers itself in breathing
and thought stops and hesitates.
Likewise things
tugged by the moon
undergo the influence of
the tidal sigh, the malleable eclipse.
And the boats' planks
swell gently in water.

Questa pagina è una stanza disabitata.
Ogni tanto porto una seggiola rotta
o un pacco di giornali, e li abbandono
in un angolo: nient'altro.
Quello che avanza si dispone qui
e nella tregua dell'uso si deposita.
È l'ultima sosta degli oggetti
prima d'uscire dall'orizzonte della casa,
nella luce chiara del loro tramonto.

This page is a room left unoccupied.
Every so often I lug in a broken chair
or a sheaf of journals and drop them
in a corner—and that's it.
Whatever's cast off here, cashiered
from use, settles itself in layers.
It's the last port of call for things
before sinking beneath the house's horizon
in the clear light of their own sunset.

La penna non dovrebbe mai lasciare
la mano di chi scrive.
Ormai ne è un osso, un dito.
Come un dito gratta, afferra ed indica.
È un ramo del pensiero
e dà i suoi frutti:
offre riparo ed ombra.

The pen should never leave
the hand that writes.
With time it grows into a bone, a finger.
Fingerlike, it scratches, clutches, points.
It's a branch of thought
and yields its own fruits,
offers shelter and shade.

Foglio bianco
come la cornea d'un occhio.
Io m'appresto a ricamarvi
un'iride e nell'iride incidere
il profondo gorgo della retina.
Lo sguardo allora
germinerà dalla pagina
e s'aprirà una vertigine
in questo quadernetto giallo.

The white page
like the cornea of an eye.
I hurriedly embroider
an iris and in the iris etch
the deep gorge of the retina.
A gaze then
sprouts from the page
and a chasm gapes
in this yellow notebook.

Scivola la penna
verso l'inguine della pagina,
ed in silenzio si raccoglie la scrittura.
Questo foglio ha i confini geometrici
di uno stato africano, in cui dispongo
i filari paralleli delle dune.
Ormai sto disegnando
mentre racconto ciò
che raccontando si profila.
È come se una nube
arrivasse ad avere
forma di nube.

The pen slips
toward the page's crotch
and the writing silently emerges
in the complex figure
of an African state, in which I arrange
the parallel stripes of sand dunes.
And by this stage I'm drawing
while I tell what
being told comes into being.
It's as though a cloud
should have taken on
the shape of a cloud.

Nel letto aggrovigliate
stanno le mie radici di carne,
solo la testa sporge
come una pianta dalla terra.
In questa esposizione alla notte
come in una marea sizigiale,
la luce si ritira e scopre
la nudità fertile dello spirito.

Tangled in the bed
are my roots of flesh,
only the head sticks out
like a plant from the earth.
In this exposure to the night
as in a syzygial tide,
the light withdraws and unveils
the spirit's fertile nudity.

Molto sottrae il sonno alla vita.
L'opera sospinta al margine del giorno
scivola lenta nel silenzio.
La mente sottratta a se stessa
si ricopre di palpebre.
E il sonno si allarga nel sonno
come un secondo corpo intollerabile.

Sleep subtracts much from life.
The work suspended at the edge of day
gradually sinks into silence.
The mind subtracted from itself
is veiled with eyelids.
And sleep grows within sleep
like a sinister second body.

A quest'ora l'occhio
rientra in se stesso.
Il corpo vorrebbe chiudersi nel cervello
per dormire.
Tutte le membra rincasano:
è tardi. E queste due ragazze
sul sedile del treno
s'inclinano col sonno nella testa
stordite dal riposo.
Sono animali al pascolo.

At this hour the eye
turns back within itself.
The body wants to shut itself inside the brain
to sleep.
All the limbs rush home.
It's late. And these two girls
seated in the train
lean into their drowsiness,
stunned by sleep.
Animals at pasture.

D'estate, come i cinema, io chiudo.
Il pensiero mi vola via e si perde,
il segno si fa vacante,
l'aria è calda
la tavola piena di frutta.

Summertime, like the cinemas, I shut up shop.
Thought flies off elsewhere and evaporates.
Billboards write white,
the air's warm,
the table weighted with fruit.

Questa pioggia di cenere
lungo i cortili gialli
fa sembrare i lenzuoli
lapidi.
Ogni panno è un sudario
in questa ora
meridiana e verticale.

This rain of ashes
on the yellow courtyards
makes the sheets
seem gravestones.
Each pegged cloth a shroud
in the vertical noon.

Esistono libri che servono
a svelare altri libri,
ma scrivere in genere è nascondere,
sottrarre alla realtà qualcosa
di cui sentirà la mancanza.
Questa maieutica del segno
indicando le cose con il loro dolore
insegna a riconoscerle.

There are some books that serve
to unveil others,
but writing's usually about spiriting away,
subtracting certain things from reality
whose loss will then be felt.
This maieutics of the sign
makes them manifest: by their travail
we learn to see them.

Spesso c'è bonaccia sulla pagina.
Inutile girarla per cercare
l'angolo del vento.
Si sta fermi,
il pensiero oscilla,
si riparano le cose
che la navigazione ha guastato.

Often the page lies becalmed.
It's futile turning it to find
what quarter the wind
might blow from.
Nothing moves.
Thought wavers in that calm.
What navigation wrecked
is there, being
painfully repaired.

Quella donna ha un potere magico:
sa fare a meno di me.
Anch'io vorrei saperne fare a meno.
Per chi mi trascura, per cosa?
Affascinato la seguo, per scoprire
nel suo nascosto affetto un affetto
che superi il mio.
Cosí un desiderio di giudice
spinge l'uomo al crimine.

That woman is possessed
of a magic power: she knows
how to do without me.
I'd also like to know
how to do without. . .
But who does she neglect me for?
For what? Intrigued,
I pursue her to uncover
in her hidden love a love
that overpowers my own.
Thus a desire for justice
spurs a man on to a life of crime.

Ma una strada interna deve esserci,
una specie di scorciatoia
tra la testa e le gambe
che attraversi braccia, stomaco
e quelle che Omero chiama
nel diciottesimo libro le vergogne.
Un sentiero appartato
immerso dentro al corpo,
una vena passata inosservata
o un fiume navigabile,
una rete tramviaria
o un sotterraneo. Un'idea
appoggiata come un ombrello
e dimenticata.

But some internal highway must exist,
a sort of shortcut
between the head and legs
crossing the arms, the stomach
and those parts which in the eighteenth book
Homer names the Shameful.
A pathway set apart,
sunk deep into the body,
a vein passed by unobserved
or a navigable waterway,
a network of tramlines
or an underground track. An idea
propped against the wall like an umbrella
and then forgotten.

Dieci poesie scritte in un mese
non è molto anche se questa
sarebbe l'undicesima.
Neanche i temi poi sono diversi
anzi c'è un solo tema
ed ha per tema il tema, come adesso.
Questo per dire quanto
resta di qua della pagina
e bussa e non può entrare,
e non deve. La scrittura
non è specchio, piuttosto
il vetro zigrinato delle docce,
dove il corpo si sgretola
e solo la sua ombra traspare
incerta ma reale.
E non si riconosce chi si lava
ma soltanto il suo gesto.
Perciò che importa
vedere dietro la filigrana,
se io sono il falsario
e solo la filigrana è il mio lavoro.

Ten poems written in one month
isn't that much to show for it
even if this would make the eleventh,
and the themes are not exactly various—
rather, there's just the one theme, which has
for its theme, as here, the theme.
Which goes to show how much
remains beyond the page,
knocks, but cannot—must not—
gain admittance. Writing's not
a mirror but rather
the shower screen's frosted glass
—behind which, real enough,
but darkly, a body
is discerned; though whose you couldn't say,
only how it moves. So why peer
behind the watermark
when I'm the counterfeiter
and only the watermark's my real work?

Di sera quando è poca la luce,
nascosto dentro il letto
colgo i profili dei ragionamenti
che scorrono sul silenzio delle membra.
È qui che devo tessere
l'arazzo del pensiero
e disponendo i fili di me stesso
disegnare con me la mia figura.
Questo non è un lavoro
ma una lavorazione.
Della carta prima, poi del corpo.
Suscitare la forma del pensiero,
sagomarla secondo una misura.
Penso ad un sarto
che sia la sua stessa stoffa.

Evenings when the light is almost nil,
holed up in bed,
I harvest the mind-cast silhouettes
that course across the silence of my limbs.
It's here that I have to embroider
thought's arras
and, spreading out the threads of my self,
out of myself design my own figure.
This isn't labor
so much as elaboration.
First of the paper, then of the body.
Drawing forth the forms thought takes,
shaping them according to a measure.
I think of a tailor
who uses himself as a roll of cloth.

Ho il cervello popolato di donne.
Da qualche parte
dev'essersi sfondato il cranio
e mormorando mi sgorga in testa
una fontana d'amore.
In questa regione d'ombra
cammino come un pellegrino
o come un monaco.
Dietro ogni curva
s'affaccia un viso silenzioso
bianco come una lapide.

My mind is full of women.
Somewhere
the dome of my skull
must be stove in
for such a stream
of murmuring,
such a fountain of love
to enter.
In this shadow land
I roam like a pilgrim
or a monk.
Round every corner,
every curve,
a silent face looks out,
pale as a gravestone.

Scrivere come se questo
fosse opera di traduzione,
di qualcosa già scritto in altra lingua.
La parola si carica ed esita,
continua ancora a vibrare
come sulla tastiera le note tenute
sopravvivono allo staccato
e lo percorrono fino al suo tacere.

To write as if this
were a work of translation,
something already penned in another language.
The word is freighted and hesitates,
still keeps vibrating
as when on a keyboard the held notes
endure beyond the detachment of touch,
keep sounding on until their silencing.

Prosegue il catalogo
delle vegetazioni.
Ecco gli arbusti e le erbe,
le specie e le differenze,
gloria botanica del pensiero,
flora d'immagini e foglie.
Come una tela
molte volte dipinta
in cui tante diverse
mani si susseguono,
cosí questo paesaggio si ripete
e assume le movenze
lente del canto gregoriano.

The catalogue of vegetation
proceeds.
Here are the shrubs and grasses,
the contrasting species,
thought's botanic refulgence.
Like a canvas,
much overpainted,
on which many different
hands have worked,
this landscape repeats itself
and assumes the slow
progress of a Gregorian chant.

FROM

NATURE E

VENATURE

1987

NATURES AND

VEININGS

1987

La febbre mi solleva verso il caldo
come una leva che per fulcro avesse
il mio polso sinistro.
Qui sta il numero
esatto di quei battiti
da cui sono infiammato
e che mi fanno alzare nella notte
come un drago cinese
di carta
incandescente ed istoriato.

Fever
lifts me up toward the heat
like a lever
whose fulcrum is
my own
left wrist
—within which are the exact
number of those beats
that overheat me
and make me rise in the night
like a Chinese
paper dragon:
lurid, incandescent.

FIBONACCI

Osservo il panorama della fronte
nella sua piena nudità,
nel numero, lo stesso, che produce
la crescita dei rami,
la facciata leggera di una chiesa,
le spire della chiocciola,
le foglie.

I note the forehead's curvature
in its utter nakedness
and deduce the same number
that underwrites
how branches grow,
a church's poised façade,
the snail-shell spiral,
and the form of leaves.

Ho spesso immaginato che gli sguardi
sopravvivano all'atto del vedere
come fossero aste,
tragitti misurati, lance
in una battaglia.
Allora penso che dentro una stanza
appena abbandonata
simili tratti debbano restare
qualche tempo sospesi ed incrociati
nell'equilibrio del loro disegno
intatti e sovrapposti come i legni
dello shangai.

I've often imagined that looks
outlive the act of seeing
as though they were poles
with measurable trajectories, lances
hurled in a battle.
Then I think that in a room
just left, lines
of this kind must stay
for some time poised
crisscross, crosshatched,
upholding their structure
like pickup sticks.

Una barca è una leva e niente è piú bello di una barca.
SIMONE WEIL

Una città volante, semovente,
in bilico su un bosco
di palafitte, mobile
nell'incanto del peso,
nella grazia della distribuzione,
inclinata,
oscillante in un leggero tremito, un attrito
che la consuma. Lungo i suoi canali
pieni di frutta, carichi di macedonia,
passano barche dalle chiglie deformi
come colonne vertebrali, tòrte
dall'acqua, oblique,
equilibrate appena.

A boat is a lever, and nothing's lovelier than a boat.

SIMONE WEIL

A flying city on autopilot,
poised upon a forest
of stakes, moving in accord
with the enchantment
of its own weight, with the grace
of its distribution,
leaning,
wavering in a faint tremor, a friction
that will erode it. All along its canals
laden with fruit, with fruit salads,
pass boats whose keels are skewed like
spinal columns, twisted
by water, out of kilter,
barely managing to balance.

E la crepa nella tazza apre
un sentiero alla terra dei morti

W. H. AUDEN

. . . come quando una crepa
attraversa una tazza

R. M. RILKE

Ricevo da te questa tazza
rossa per bere ai miei giorni
uno ad uno
nelle mattine pallide, le perle
della lunga collana della sete.
E se cadrà rompendosi, distrutto,
io, dalla compassione,
penserò a ripararla,
per proseguire i baci ininterrotti.
E ogni volta che il manico
o l'orlo si incrineranno
tornerò a incollarli
finché il mio amore non avrà compiuto
l'opera dura e lenta del mosaico.

You gave me this red cup
from which to drink to my days on earth
one by one
in the pallid mornings, the pearls
strung on thirst's long necklace.
And should it fall and crack,
stunned by regret,
I'll have to mend it
so as to keep unbroken
that sequence of kisses.
And each time the round
of handle or rim
chips, I'll glue it back
until my love
has finished
the slow, hard graft of a mosaic.

Scende lungo il declivio
candido della tazza
lungo l'interno concavo
e luccicante, simile alla folgore,
la crepa,
nera, fissa,
segno di un temporale
che continua a tuonare
sopra il paesaggio sonoro,
di smalto.

Right down the dip of the cup's white slope,
along the clear curved inside,
like a jag of lightning,
fixed and black,
the crack descends
—sign of a storm
whose thunder still echoes
over this landscape
of glazed resonance.

Antaura era il nome neoplatonico del
maledetto e diabolico demone dell'emicrania.

A. A. BARB

L'emicrania si approssima, rullano
i tamburi, dalla parte di sotto,
dall'emisfero notturno.
Spuntano le tribú,
le sue costellazioni
montano, piumata coda
della bestia inferiore.
Salgono su dal basso, appaiono
mentre la terra risuona dall'interno
percossa e cava, vivente
timpano.

Antaura was the Neoplatonic name for the
accursed and diabolic demon of the migraine.

A. A. BARB

Drumrolls from the depths,
from night's hemisphere,
herald the migraine.
Tribes, constellations
break out, their crests rear up
with the plumed tail
of the beast from below
while the world's inner walls
clang and resound,
hollowed out, percussive,
a living eardrum.

Se per chiamarti devo fare un numero
tu ti trasformi in numero,
disponi i lineamenti
nella combinazione a cui rispondi.
Il tre che si ripete,
il nove al terzo posto,
indicano qualcosa del tuo volto.
Quando ti cerco
devo disegnare la tua figura,
devo fare nascere le sette cifre
analoghe al tuo nome
finché non si dischiuda la cassa-
forte della viva voce.

Di colpo, mentre sto telefonando,
l'interferenza altera il dialogo,
lo moltiplica, apre una prospettiva
dentro lo spazio buio
dell'udito.
Mi vedo verticale, sonnambolico,
in bilico su una fuga di voci
gemelle, allacciate una all'altra,
sorprese nel contatto.

If I have to use digits to call you,
you undergo a transformation
into digits, your lineaments mutate
to the number that gets through to you.
The double three,
then the nine that comes third,
recall something in your face.
When in search of you
I have to draw up your figure,
I have to spawn the seven ciphers
that are analogues of your name
until the combination safe
of your living voice
unlocks itself.

All of a sudden, while I'm on the phone,
some static rucks our voices,
multiplies them, springs open a long view
within hearing's
dark space.
I catch an image of myself vertical, a sleepwalker
suspended above a fugue of voices,
twin sisters, bound one to the other,
stunned by the contact.

Sento la lingua della bestia ctònia,
l'orrida treccia di parole, frasi, il mostro
policefalo e difforme che chiama me
dalle profondità.

I hear the tongue of the ancient creature
from the underworld,
the hideous braided words and phrases,
the monster who,
misshapen, many-headed, calls me
from the deep.

Nei disegni dei bambini
colpisce la violenza delle linee.
La mente sembra crescere di sghembo
portandosi via la matita.
Tutto è storto e perenne
o forse soltanto piegato
come quando scendendo nell'acqua
pare spezzarsi il remo.

Il giocattolo si fa incontro
uscito dal gioco per mostrarsi
estraneo all'estraneo.
Anche l'infanzia torna
ostile e trasformata
come quella di un altro.
Le sue tracce appartengono
solamente a se stessa,
alla natura fossile del bimbo.

In children's drawings
the violence of the lines
is what's striking. The mind seems
to have grown crooked,
carried away by the crayon.
Everything's forever twisted
or perhaps only bent
as when dipping in water
the oar appears broken.

The toy stands out,
has left the game to show itself
alien to the alien.
Even childhood returns
hostile, altered,
like someone else's.
Its traces belong
to itself alone,
to the fossil nature of the child.

Voglio poter un giorno
esser marmorizzato
senza piú nervature
o fili di tendini o vene.
Soltanto malta aerea, nubilosa,
calce spenta, la tunica
striata da un vento
che non soffia.

I should like, one day,
to be turned to marble,
to be stripped of nerves,
glistening tendons, veins.
Just to be airy enamel,
slaked lime, the striped
tunic of a wind
ground to a halt.

Una scissura,
la stessa che riga le forme
stampate nella plastica,
divide me in due versanti.
Un lato manovra
con naturalezza
aderendo all'impulso, è l'impulso,
azione felice.
L'altro è inetto,
l'infermo che patisce
senza guarire mai,
lo spazio convalescente.
Anche in certe condanne
il vivo veniva legato a un cadavere,
ma non al suo cadavere. Dunque
questa paralisi che affligge metà
corpo, sembra il motivo
dell'inclinazione
e della pendenza dell'anima.

A groove
like the vertical join
in plastic figurines
cuts me in two, two sides,
two slopes. One side moves
instinctively—a natural—
guided by impulse, being just
that: the felicitous act.
The other's hopeless,
an invalid that suffers
without ever recovering:
a convalescent space.
Punishments have been devised
where the live person is tied
to a corpse, though not
in that case
his own corpse. So
this paralysis that strikes
one half of the body
would seem to explain
the soul's angle of inclination,
its gradient and overhang.

Quante arie ascoltate una volta
proseguono il loro cammino,
stanno nella memoria,
ne solcano lo spazio. Nel legno
dei violini l'esame radiografico
mostra l'intrico dei tarli
filiforme, mobile, cava
chioma serpentina, irraggiante
di vene che percorrono e minano
l'interno delle fibre.
E tramata di musica la testa
si fa leggera e vuota, di merletto.

How many tunes, heard once only,
which follow their own promptings,
which we can't get out of our heads,
which furrow the space there. In the wood
of violins X-rays show up
the intricate damage,
a snaky, shifting, threaded
coiffure rayed out with veins
that weave across and excavate
the fibrous interior.
So worm-eaten with music,
we become light-headed, empty-headed,
as if made of fine lace.

Non sono di nessuno
le terrazze condominiali.
Vi si lasciano i panni
ad asciugare,
i panni del deserto.
Sono altopiani vasti,
vasti e disabitati,
abbandonati ad un'infanzia aerea.

They belong to no one,
the balconies of blocks of flats.
Washing is left out
there to dry like
linen in the desert.
They're highland planes,
vast uninhabited zones,
left to fend for themselves
in their aerial infancy.

ROSEBUD

Non pretendo di dire la parola
che scoccata dal cuore traversi
le dodici scuri forate
fino a forare il cuore del pretendente.
Io traccio il mio bersaglio
intorno all'oggetto colpito,
io non colgo nel segno ma segno
ciò che colgo, baro,
scelgo il mio centro dopo il tiro
e come con un'arma difettosa
di cui conosco ormai
lo scarto, adesso
miro alla mira.

I make no claim to speak the word
that shot from the heart can travel through
the twelve pierced axes
before it strikes the suitor's heart.
I trace my target out
in a circle around the object struck.
I make my mark out of the mark I've made:
whatever I hit. —I cheat,
choosing the bull's-eye after the shot's fired
and as though handling a faulty weapon
of which by this stage
I know the exact degree
of deviation, now
I have the sight in my sights.

Non avere da scrivere nulla
dà quella pena infantile, infinita,
di chi non trova alloggio
in un paese straniero.
Si cerca ovunque,
ogni posto è già occupato,
provate altrove e intanto
si fa tardi e non c'è verso.
Dove andremo a dormire?

Having nothing to write
causes that same boundless
childlike foreboding
as being unable to find
a bed abroad.
You look high and low
but every room's already booked.
You try elsewhere but meanwhile
it's gotten late and there's no
hint or hope of an opening.
So where will we find a place to sleep?

La spiaggia, il legno fradicio, i copertoni
gonfi e le bottiglie, cose
guaste e corrotte, tutto questo
mi è caro, ciò che resta astenuto,
rimesso, senza scopo,
ciò che nessuno ruba,
ciò che avanza.
D'aprile
l'aria si fa appena calda.
Pare una guancia.

On the beach, rotten wood, tires, bottles,
sodden stuff—all things wrecked
and putrified—I love them all:
what's washed up, spewed out, good-for-nothing,
what no one wants
to have or filch.
In April the air
takes on a hint of warmth.
Glows like a cheek.

Si sta sopra il pontile
come su una rovina,
un ponte
che porta alle acque.

You stand on the pier
as though on a ruin,
a bridge that gives
onto the waters.

Il sonno interrotto stride,
fischia, ramo spezzato,
legna verde, vergine,
che cede di netto
ma i cui tronconi restano uniti
da qualche bianca fibra lunga
inerme nascosta nell'interno,
l'anima della pianta,
il tendine.

Interrupted sleep whistles and creaks,
a snapped branch that bares
green virgin wood—it's broken clean
but the sundered parts remain
held together
by a long white fiber,
meek, shivering, undefended,
the plant's heart and soul,
its tendon.

Passato qualche tempo tutto il latte
va a male, come se andasse verso
il male, la sua cattività,
si contrae, si rapprende,
abbandona il proprio stato liquido
e inizia a farsi forma.
La sostanza rafferma
prende corpo, resuscita
in una carne nuova e compatta, estratta
dalla bestia. È cacio, metamorfosi
del secreto animale, il frutto
morto di una pianta viva,
sazia creatura pallida e lunare.

With the passage of time all the milk
goes bad, as though
it had turned evil.
It contracts, solidifies,
sloughs off its proper liquid form,
assumes a body, revived
in new compact flesh, extracted
from the beast. It turns to
cheese, a metamorphosis
of an animal secretion, the dead
fruit off a living plant,
a pale sated lunar being.

La luce della luna è lavorata ad arte,
una materia prima profilata, tornita
fino ad essere pietra
focaia, fiamma minerale,
ma fiamma fioca, morta, come l'erba
fatta crescere al buio,
la pallida, rituale veccia,
che dà il chiarore fosforescente,
freddo e subacqueo
dell'acetilene.

The moonlight is a work of art,
a substance first outlined, then polished
till it's flintstone, mineral flame,
but flame that's enfeebled, dead, like grass
grown in the dark,
a pale ritual vetch
whose glow has the cold
submerged phosphorescence
of acetylene.

Con ingranaggi, lancette, dentature,
l'orologio sembra un carro falcato
che fa scempio del giorno, ne dilania
la salma, lede i legami e le giunture,
trincia le ore, le disossa, come
la rotazione della notte strappa
la chiarità del cielo e mette a nudo
numeri, membrature, figure,
lo scheletro brillante
e nebuloso delle costellazioni.
Cosí, radiografato, il corpo
si ritira, nella bassa marea,
scopre i fondali, le terre
sottostanti, le montagne,
i fossili dormienti
sotto la carnagione della luce.

With cogs, tiny levers, and teeth,
the clock seems a chariot armed with scythes
to rip the day to bits—it rends
the day's corpse, tears its joints and tendons,
shreds the hours, bones them, as night's
rotation uproots
the sky's light and strips bare
numbers, figures, frameworks,
the shining cloudy skeleton
of the constellations.
So, X-rayed, the body
retires, at low tide,
uncovers its bed, the underlying
lowlands, the mountaintops,
the dormant fossils
beneath light's healthy flesh tones.

Quanto è triste imparare troppo tardi una lingua.
Hanno chiuso le porte
e resti fuori con qualche pezzo in mano,
rotto. Domandi a cosa serve,
come funziona, se è montato bene,
ma è inutile sapere una cosa per volta. Manca
lo stampo, la pressione, il fuoco.
E incontri solamente
le parole che non conosci
o hai già dimenticato.
Io temo che il tedesco abbia perduto i nomi
e i verbi che so ricordare.
Forse sono una falla
che si spalanca nei suoi dizionari.

How sad it is to learn a language too late.
They've shut the doors,
and you're left outside with a small
broken piece in your hand. You ask
what's it for, how it works, if it's well
made, but it's no use knowing things
one by one. What's missing is
the casting, the pressure, the fire.
And you only meet
words you don't know
or have already forgotten.
I have this fear that German's lost
the nouns and verbs I have by rote.
Perhaps I'm the fault, the breach
that gapes within its dictionaries.

Poiché non esce intero, luccicante,
smaltato pesce sacro, non esce.

Va diviso, segnato,
lavorato, il suo filone intatto,
la sua vena lucente nella notte
di pietra.

Ora posso dormire,
cavato il dente del giudizio,
segato in tre parti,
estratto per piccoli pezzi,
ridotto in frammenti per essere tolto.

Because it won't come out whole,
a sacred fish, enameled, all aglow,
it won't come out at all.

It has to be divided, scored, crossed,
worked on, keeping its nerve
intact, its vein shining
in a night of stone.

Now I can sleep—
rid of the wisdom tooth,
that's sawed into three parts,
pulled piece by piece,
broken down to be uprooted.

Amo i gesti imprecisi,
uno che inciampa, l'altro
che fa urtare il bicchiere,
quello che non ricorda,
chi è distratto, la sentinella
che non sa arrestare il battito
breve delle palpebre,
mi stanno a cuore
perché vedo in loro il tremore,
il tintinnio familiare
del meccanismo rotto.
L'oggetto intatto tace, non ha voce
ma solo movimento. Qui invece
ha ceduto il congegno,
il gioco delle parti,
un pezzo si separa,
si annuncia.
Dentro qualcosa balla.

Gestures that go astray
appeal to me—the one
who trips up or upturns
a glass of . . . the one who forgets,
is miles away, the sentry
with the insubordinate eyelid
—my heart goes out
to all of them, all who betray
the unmistakable
whirr and clunk
of the busted contraption.
Things that work are muffled
and mute—their parts just move.
Here instead the gadgetry,
the mesh of cogs, has given up
the ghost—a bit sticks out,
breaks off, declares itself.
Inside, something throbs.

97

Qual è la sinistra della parola,
come si muove nello spazio,
dove proietta la sua ombra
(ma può una parola fare ombra?),
come osservarne il retro
o poggiarla di scorcio?
Mi piacerebbe rendere in poesia
l'equivalente della prospettiva pittorica.
Dare ad un verso la profondità del coniglio
che scappa tra i campi e renderlo distante
mentre già si allontana da chi osserva
dirigendosi verso la cornice
sempre piú piccolo
ma fermo tuttavia.
La campagna lo osserva,
e si dispone intorno all'animale,
al punto che la fugge.

Which is the left-hand side of the word?
How does it move about in space?
Where does it throw its shadow
(and can a word cast shadow)?
How can it be observed from behind
or set against the recession of space?
I should like to render in poetry
the equivalent of perspective in painting.
To give a poem the depth of a rabbit
escaping through the fields and make it
distant while already
it speeds away from the one who's watching
and veers toward the frame
becoming smaller all the time
and never budging an inch.
The countryside observes
and disposes itself around the creature,
around a point that's vanishing.

In una via fabbricavano busti di santi,
di ogni dimensione, colorati, in un'altra
solo braccia e candele dipinte, visi
racchiusi nelle immaginette, altrove
disegnavano scene di gente
salvata dalle acque, con le nuvole bianche
per scriverci la dedica, oppure lavoravano
a cuori d'argento battuto
raggiati con liste sottili,
tutte parti del corpo trasformate in gioielli,
in protesi, in corpi del reato, per adire
le vie celesti.

On one street they fashioned colored busts of saints
in every size, while on another
only arms and painted candles, faces
boxed in cramped frames; elsewhere
they drew scenes of people
saved from drowning, with white clouds
to write a message on, or else they worked
on hearts of beaten silver
rayed out with fine spokes,
every part of the body turned into jewels,
prosthetics, corpus delicti
to start proceedings
in the streets and courts of heaven.

Questa grafia si logora,
saltano gli angoli, le «erre»,
le «emme», tornano tonde,
rotolano limate, levigate
pietre nella corrente.
I volti anche,
i volti si consumano
a forza d'esser guardati.
Diventano paesaggi
di rovine.

This writing's being worn away,
its angles smoothed, the "r"s,
the "m"s, are turned
and sanded down and roll like stones
the currents shift from shore to shore.
Faces also,
faces waste away
from the pressure of being watched.
They turn into a landscape
full of ruins.

Il mio cuore è scheggiato,
scalfita
la superficie scintillante
e dura dello smalto, quel manto
freddo, metallizzato,
lucido, delicato prodotto
della verniciatura a fuoco.

Sto solo come un chiodo
insieme alla sua ombra.
Solo come un proiettile
che non fa in tempo
a proiettare ombra.

Filare sospeso a mezz'aria
sui 180 all'ora.
Passare sulle cose
sfiorandole,
toccandole appena,
ma già lontano,
già troppo lontano
per sentire il rumore che fanno
cadendo.

My heart's been chipped,
its hard enameled surface nicked
and keyed—that coat of light,
cold and metallized, was frail:
the product and effect
of fired paint.

I'm solitary as a nail
nailed to its shadow,
lone as a bullet
that hasn't time
to cast a shadow.

Hurtling through the air
at over a hundred,
barely touching
the things
I pass over
but already too far,
too far on to hear
the noise they make
as they collapse.

GIUNGLA D'ASFALTO

Vagano nella notte
vasti gli autobus,
anime in pena,
scrigni di luce pallida,
tremanti, vuoti, utili
soltanto a chi è lontano,
avanti e indietro
sempre legati ad una linea
di dolore,
e lasciano salire ad ogni sosta
un sospiro
che sembra una preghiera.

They rove through the night—
these now huge buses,
souls in torment,
treasure chests that leak
tired light,
trembling, empty, useful
only to those
way off, at a far remove;
back and forth they rove,
forever bound
to a line
of grief,
at every stop
delivered of
a sigh
that seems a prayer.

I sospiri, i sorrisi del telefono
non vogliono risposta.
È la voce che luccica,
che vale,
che tintinnando saluta
per chiedere il suo equivalente
al modo in cui si cambia del denaro
in moneta straniera.

Il telefono è il mio rubinetto
la fontana di voci, la doccia,
l'acqua è sempre la stessa,
ma la goccia
ogni volta è diversa. Pensa ai poveri
granelli di carbone
che danzano una danza
nuova ad ogni respiro
mai la stessa, i volatili, i passeri
che intorno a questa vasca
saltellano perché noi ci parliamo.

Sighs and smiles on the telephone
ask no reply
—it's the voice that shines forth,
that counts,
that, tinkling, greets
and holds out for a fair exchange
the way that money's turned
to foreign currency.

The telephone is my tap,
fountain of voices, shower.
The water's always the same
but each drop's
distinct. Think of the poor
carbon grains
that dance a different
dance with every breath
renewed—the winged ones, the sparrows
that hop around this birdbath
just because we're talking.

Io cammino fumando
e dopo ogni boccata
attraverso il mio fumo
e sto dove non stavo
dove prima soffiavo.

While I'm walking I smoke
and with each toke I take
I cleave through my smoke
to arrive where I wasn't
myself yet present
where my smoke had been sent.

FROM

ESERCIZI DI

TIPTOLOGIA

1992

TYPTOLOGICAL

EXERCISES

1992

Che la materia provochi il contagio
se toccata nelle sue fibre ultime
recisa come il vitello dalla madre
come il maiale dal proprio cuore
stridendo nel vedere le sue membra strappate;

Che tale schianto generi
la stessa energia che divampa
quando la società si lacera, sacro velo del tempio
e la testa del re cade spiccata dal corpo dello stato
affinché il taumaturgo diventi la ferita;

Che l'abbraccio del focolare sia radiazione
rogo della natura che si disgrega
inerme davanti al sorriso degli astanti
per offrire un lievissimo aumento
della temperatura ambientale;

Che la forma di ogni produzione
implichi effrazione, scissione, un addio
e la storia sia l'atto del combúrere
e la Terra una tenera catasta di legname
messa a asciugare al sole,

è incredibile, no?

That matter engenders contagion
if interfered with in its deepest fibers
cut out from its mother like a veal calf
like the pig from its own heart
screaming at the sight of its torn entrails;

That this destruction generates
the same energy that blazes out
when society turns on itself, the temple's veil torn
and the king's head axed from the body of the state
until the faith healer becomes the wound;

That the hearth's embrace is radiation,
nature's pyre, which unravels
helplessly before the smiling company
so as to effect the slightest increase
of the surrounding temperature;

That the form of every production implies
breaking and entry, fission, a final leavetaking,
and that history is the act of combustion
and the Earth a tender stockpile of firewood
left out to dry in the sun,

is hard to credit, is it not?

XOCHIMILCO

Mi costruisco su una colonna assente.

H. MICHAUX

Le bende, barbe delle piante, tenere
fluttuano giú nel basso
congiungendosi al morbido,
al cieco, all'intatto del fondale,
congiungendosi a me.
Giunche che sono terra, zattere,
lingue tremule al battere dei flutti.
La mia fondazione fu rituale
e insensata, e sorsi sul franare
e nacqui dal mancare
palafitta del nulla
palo nel nulla fitto.

XOCHIMILCO

I build myself upon an absent column.

HENRI MICHAUX

Bindings, bandages, plants' beards
waft downward to the depths,
unite themselves with the soft,
the blind, the untouched,
echo-located abyss,
unite themselves with me.
Out of reeds is this earth made
—rafts, their bindings loosed, tongues
wagging to the pulse of wavelets.
My founding was ritual,
insentient—I spired from
a landspill, was born
from an ache, a lack;
pileworks, pickup sticks, interstices,
a stake stuck in the void.

APERÇU

Solo la folle escrescenza.

O. MANDELSTAM

Il verme solitario, il parassita,
lo scroccone e il saprofita,
il cancro, nascono da organismi
che covano la propria fine
come la musica dell'Occidente.
Prima la gemmazione
di timide dissonanze, poi le metastasi
che invadono il corpo sonoro e lo disgregano,
corruzione mirabile e frutteto
di morte. È la storia di una catastrofe tonale,
cellule a-ritmiche, superfetazioni,
ossia il Dirottatore (e il cancro
dirotta sempre il suo veicolo).
Ecco la terra, povero velivolo
preso in ostaggio da un passeggero armato.

APERÇU

Only the mad excrescence.
OSIP MANDELSTAM

The tapeworm, the parasite,
the scrounger, the saprophyte,
cancer: they're born from organisms
that conceal their own ends
like the music of the West.
First the budding
of timid dissonance, then the metastases
that invade the sonorous body and break it down,
admirable corruption and orchard
of death. It's the history of a tonal catastrophe,
arrhythmic cells, superfetations,
or else of a hijacker (and cancer
always hijacks its own vehicle).
And here's the Earth, poor aircraft
taken hostage by an armed passenger.

HELGOLAND

Una lastra di pietra immersa nell'acqua, inclinata
dolcemente verso la Gran Bretagna, rampa di lancio
verdissima, brughiere e covi di U-Booten,
cava e cariata, isola e arsenale mimetico.
Poi, conquistata, cancellarla via, grattarla dalle carte
geografiche sfregando con l'ovatta il bollino argentato,
come per controllare se si vince qualcosa. Il tritolo
risuona per mesi nel cavo dell'inverno, soffia
sul Mare del Nord, e dentro, e sotto, finché il villaggio
viene segato in due. Ora, sul taglio delle nuove scogliere
(nuove di zecca, fresche di conio nel fervere
del bricolage litoraneo), la sua storia sta iscritta negli strati
a vista. Sotto l'erba, le maioliche di qualche cucina, asfalto,
salottini, condutture e cablati
in una dolce lezione di anatomia all'aperto, aperta
ai quattro venti.
Ma il progetto si arresta, l'esplosivo non basta,
meglio il turismo. Ed ecco il duty-free, questi negozi
porto franco, e l'isola sdoganata, tarlata, maneggiata, limata,
sagomata seggiola zoppicante, cartuccia da buttare e dunque
BOSSOLO,
disco intaccato, rimasto a galleggiare
nelle mille medaglie-souvenir.

A stone slab immersed and gently tilted
toward the U.K., a launchpad
of brightest green, warren and U-boat den,
riddled, hollowed out, island and concealed arsenal.
Then, defeated, it must be canceled out, rubbed off
the atlas like a silver scratch-card scraped by a coin
to see if we'll win something. TNT
roars for months in the cave of winter, blows
across the North Sea, within and under, till the village
is sawed in half. Now on the brand-new profile
of the rockscape (freshly minted in the sheer
excitement of this shoreline bricolage) its history
is inscribed in the exposed layers. Beneath the grass,
some kitchen tiles, asphalt, a sitting room,
strands of sprangled wires, furnish a fitting
anatomy lesson in the open air, open
to the four winds.
But the plan ground to a halt, and where explosives failed,
tourism succeeded. And here they are—the standard string
of duty-free shops, the island a market,
worm-eaten, sand-blasted and manhandled into
the shape of a chair that limps, a spent projectile aka
SHELL CASE,
a dented disc left to float
among the thousand medal-souvenirs.

PARLANO

C'è intorno una tale quiete che quasi si
può udire il tintinnare di un cucchiaino
che cade in Finlandia.

I. BRODSKIJ

Ma perché sempre dietro la mia parete?
Sempre dietro, le voci, sempre
quando scende la notte iniziano
a parlare, latrano o addirittura credono
che sussurrare sia meglio. (Mentre mi sento
questo filo d'aria fredda delle loro parole
che mi gela, che mi lega
e mi tormenta nel sonno).
Ai confini del circolo polare
una coppia piangeva nella sua stanza
oltre un muro trasparente, piangeva, luminoso,
tenero come fosse la membrana di un timpano.
(Mentre io vibravo, cassa
armonica della loro storia). Fino a che a casa mia
hanno rifatto il tetto, le tubature,
la facciata, tutto, e battevano
ovunque, sopra, sotto, e battevano sempre
chiacchierando tra loro solo quando dormivo,
solo perché dormivo,
soltanto perché fossi cassa armonica
delle loro storie.

THEY TALK

Such is the silence that one can hear the tinkle
of a teaspoon falling in Finland.

JOSEPH BRODSKY

But why's it always behind my walls?
Always there, the voices, always
when night falls
they start to talk. They bark. Or even think
whispering's better. (While I can feel their
words become this thread of air
that chills me and chokes me and breaks
my sleep up.) At the polar circle's brink
a couple wept together in their room,
beyond a wall they wept
—its luminous membrane
tender as a drumskin
or an eardrum.
(While I resounded—the sound box
of their story.) Till they started in on
the roof at my place, the whole thing, the guttering,
battering away at the front, the back,
the top, the bottom, always battering
and chattering away together only when I slept,
only because I slept,
only because I was always
the sound box
of their stories.

SUL NOME DI UN'UTILITARIA DELLA DDR CHE IN TEDESCO SIGNIFICA «SATELLITE»

Satelliti di un sistema solare che si disfa,
di un nucleo che decade, libera particelle
e perde le sue perle dai fili di orbitali, chicchi
di un ticchettío che grandinando
brillano sugli asfalti occidentali,
TRABANT rosa, beige, verde
pastello, carrozzine due tempi, tintinnanti
trabiccoli azzurrini, trine tremule,
TRABIS, patrie portatili, gingilli
di una classe fossile e stilizzata,
scatolette di latta in cui si accalca
una trepida, dolce borghesia comunista, reperti
minerali, auto di Topolino
che fuggite dal vostro pifferaio assassino,

ben arrivati ad Hameln, BRD!

ON THE NAME OF A CUV FROM THE D.D.R. THAT IN GERMAN MEANS ''SATELLITE''

Satellites of a solar system that is falling apart,
of a nucleus that releases particles
and loses its pearls from the strings of orbital masses, stones
of a hailstorm that, ticking,
shines on the asphalted West:
Trabants—pink, beige, and pastel
green, two-stroke tin tubs, tinkling
pale blue jalopies, trembling trines,
"Trabis," portable nations, knicknacks
of a fossilized and stylized class,
little tin cans in which are stashed
a fearful and meek Communist bourgeoisie, mineral
exhibits, Mickey Mouse cars
in flight from your paid killer of a pied piper,

welcome to Hamelin, B.R.D.!

PORTA WESTFALICA

Una giornata di nuvole, a Minden,
su un taxi che mi porta
in cerca di queste due parole.
Chiedo in giro e nessuno sa
cosa indichino—esattamente, dico—
che luogo sia, dove, se una fortezza
o una chiusa. Eppure il nome brilla
sulla carta geografica, un barbaglio,
nel fitto groviglio consonantico, che lancia
brevi vocali luminose, come l'arma
di un uomo in agguato nel bosco.
Si tradisce, e io vengo a cercarlo.
Il panorama op-art si squaderna tra alberi
e acque, mentre i cartelli indicano ora
una torre di Bismarck, ora il mausoleo di Guglielmo,
la statua con la gamba sinistra istoriata
dalla scritta: «Manuel war da»,
incisa forse con le chiavi di casa, tenue
filo dorato sul verde del bronzo,
linea sinuosa della firma, fiume
tra fiumi. Lascio la macchina, inizio a camminare.
Foglie morte, una luce mobile, l'aria gelata,
la fitta di una storta alla caviglia,
io, trottola che prilla, io,
vite che si svita. Nient'altro.
Eppure qui sta il segno, qui

One cloudy day, at Minden,
in a taxi that takes me
in search of these two words.
I ask around and no one knows
what they stand for—my point exactly, I reply—
what kind of place is it and where, and whether
fortress or lock. Still, the name shines
on the map, emits a blaze in the tight knot
of consonants that give off short
luminous vowels like the weapon
of a man lying in wait in the wood.
He gives himself away and I go to hunt him down.
The op-art panorama opens up between trees
and waters, while the signs point out now
a tower of Bismarck, now William's mausoleum,
the statue with its left leg emblazoned
with the words "Manuel war da,"
chiseled maybe with his house keys, a tenuous
gold thread on the bronze's verdigris,
the sinuous line of the signature, a river
among rivers. I leave the car and start to walk.
Dead leaves, shifting light and frozen air.
The pang of a twisted ankle. I am
a spinning top, a screw
that's been unscrewed. There's nothing else.
Yet here is the sign, here the earth

si strozza la terra,
qui sta il by-pass, il muro
di una Berlino idrica in mezzo
a falde freatiche, bacini artificiali,
e la pace e la guerra e la lingua latina.
Niente. E mentre giro nella foresta penso
all'autista che attende perplesso,
all'autista che attende perplesso
e ne approfitta per lavare i vetri
mentre nel suo brusío
sotto il cruscotto scorre sussurrando
il fiume del tassametro, l'elica del denaro,
diga, condotto, sbocco, chiusa dischiusa, aorta,
emorragia del tempo e valvola mitralica,
Porta Westfalica della vita mia.

throttles itself, here is the bypass, the wall
of a watery Berlin in the midst of
phreatic strata, man-made basins,
war and peace and the Latin language.
Nothing. And wandering in the forest, I think
of the driver who waits and frets,
of the driver who waits and frets
and takes this opportunity to clean the car windows
while with a chittering sound
under the dashboard the meter runs on
like a brook, the propeller of money,
dike, conduit, outlet, opened lock, aorta,
hemorrhage of time and mitral valve,
Porta Westfalica of my life.

Dopo avere guidato qualche ora
guardo il volto
del mio interlocutore
e vedo che i suoi tratti si divaricano,
continuano ad aprirsi nella fuga
di una strada alberata.
Fammi da strada, adesso!
Mentre mi parli
io sfreccio nello spazio
incontrastato
del tuo volto.

The long drive over,
I stare ahead
at the face of this person
I'm talking to.
And the features peel
apart on either side
—a tree-lined boulevard—
in one continuous
opening out of space.
You be my street!
And when you start
to talk I just
keep hurtling on
through pure
unobstructed
miles of face.

L'ABBRACCIO

Tu dormi accanto a me cosí io mi inchino
e accostato al tuo viso prendo sonno
come fa lo stoppino
da uno stoppino che gli passa il fuoco.
E i due lumini stanno
mentre la fiamma passa e il sonno fila.
Ma mentre fila vibra
la caldaia nelle cantine.
Laggiú si brucia una natura fossile,
là in fondo arde la Preistoria, morte
torbe sommerse, fermentate,
avvampano nel mio termosifone.
In una buia aureola di petrolio
la cameretta è un nido riscaldato
da depositi organici, da roghi, da liquami.
E noi, stoppini, siamo le due lingue
di quell'unica torcia paleozoica.

As you lie beside me I edge closer,
taking sleep from your lips
as one wick draws flame from another.
And two night-lights are lit
as the flame takes and sleep passes
between us. But as it passes
the boiler in the basement shudders:
down there a fossil nature burns,
down in the depths prehistory's
sunken fermented peats blaze up
and slither through my radiator.
Wreathed in a dark halo of oil,
the bedroom is a close nest
heated by organic deposits,
by log pyres, leafmash, seething resins . . .
And we are the wicks, the two tongues
flickering on that single Paleozoic torch.

L'IMBALLATORE

Cos'è la traduzione? Su un vassoio
la testa pallida e fiammante d'un poeta . . .
    V. NABOKOV

L'imballatore chino
che mi svuota la stanza
fa il mio stesso lavoro.
Anch'io faccio cambiare casa
alle parole, alle parole
che non sono mie,
e metto mano a ciò
che non conosco senza capire
cosa sto spostando.
Sto spostando me stesso
traducendo il passato in un presente
che viaggia sigillato
racchiuso dentro pagine
o dentro casse con la scritta
«Fragile» di cui ignoro l'interno.
È questo il futuro, la spola, il traslato,
il tempo manovale e citeriore,
trasferimento e tropo,
la ditta di trasloco.

THE MOVER

What is translation? On a platter
A poet's pale and glaring head . . .
VLADIMIR NABOKOV

The weighed-down mover
who empties my room
does the same work as me.
I, too, arrange house moves
for words, for words
that aren't mine,
and lay hands on
what's beyond me
without quite figuring out
what it is I'm moving.
I am moving myself,
translating the past into a present
that travels sealed
and folded in pages
or in boxes labeled FRAGILE,
about whose contents I can only guess.
And this is the future, the shuttle
shifting back and forth, the metaphor,
laborer time, time with its hither zone,
its middle west or east,
transfer and trope,
the moving firm.

135

Ero sul letto di un ambulatorio,
nascosto dietro un paravento.
«Antigone», «Sí», «Sei qui?», «Sí, qui».
Le vertebre, le vertebre.
E iniziano a discorrere tra loro,
due vecchi, due voci di vecchi.
Perché una voce invecchia,
anche nel suono sta l'osso del tempo
anche nel fiato. Soffiavano, e c'era
dentro un'eco di se stessa,
un'eco che precedeva la pronuncia.
Qualcosa di scassato e scardinato, il midollo
sfilato dalla spina dorsale e
sguainato come una spada luccicante,
voce-carcassa
vertebra della voce.

I was lying on an outpatient's bed
hidden behind a screen.
"Antigone," "Yes," "You there?" "Yes, here."
The bones of the back, the backbone.
And they start talking to each other,
the two old folk, the two old voices.
Because a voice grows old,
even in sounds you find the bone of time,
even in breathing. They sighed and inside
the sound, the sound echoed itself,
an echo preceding the words themselves.
Something wrecked and unhinged, the marrow
stripped from the spinal column and
unsheathed like a glittering sword,
voice-carcass,
backbone of the voice.

LEZIONE DI METRICA

Un pettine d'acciaio fila
le note, sfila
una musica dolce di zucchero
filato. Come un incantatore
di serpenti incantato
mi ipnotizza la lingua
del suono che si srotola
mentre i denti di ferro,
il rosario di uncini,
strappano questa carne
da scortico, e sbranato
sta il cuore di chi ascolta.
Qui suonano il mio cuore!
Vezzo e lezzo. Rotto l'involucro
con la ballerina, il carillon si arresta
perché il cattivo gusto
è il suo buon guscio armonico,
l'astuccio per la perla
matta della leziosità. Notte.
Il violino di Frankenstein mi chiama.
E io sono quel mostro musicale
condannato alla ruota musicale
della sua musicale nostalgia.

A steel comb unpicks
the notes and trickles
a music like threads
of cotton candy. Like
a snake charmer, charmed
himself, I fall under the spell
of the tongue of sound
that unravels while
the teeth of metal,
the rosary of hooks,
rips this flesh in strips
and the listener's heart
is flayed.
It's my heart they're playing here!
Syrup and stench. When the outside
with the ballerina's broken,
the music box stops dead
because bad taste requires
its own fine tuning,
the jewel case for the wild pearl
of affectation. Night falls.
Frankenstein's violin calls me.
And I'm that musical monster
condemned to the musical wheel
of his musical nostalgia.

DIDASCALIE PER

LA LETTURA DI

UN GIORNALE

1999

INSTRUCTIONS

FOR READING

A NEWSPAPER

1999

DATA

Si comincia da qua,
luce di stella morta
giunta da un trapassato presente.
Il suo oggi è lo ieri, luce-salma,
memoria di un oltretomba quotidiano.

It begins here:
light of a dead star
that has reached us from the pluperfect present.
Its today is yesterday, corpse light,
the memory trace of a daily afterlife.

PREZZO

Iscritto nel frontone del tempio,
si dispiega in lire e in ampi
fregi di valute straniere.
Stampa per stampa, la cartamoneta
serve a acquistare una moneta-carta
il cui valore magico scade in ventiquattr'ore,
quando alla mezzanotte la fiammante
carrozza delle ultimissime ritorna
zucca, notizia avariata,
denaro fuoricorso, cartastraccia,
carcassa della cronaca,
carogna già spolpata.

Inscribed on the temple's pediment
it unfurls itself in *lire* and the broad
frieze of foreign currencies.
Print for print, paper money
serves for the acquisition of a money paper
whose magic value runs out in twenty-four hours,
when at midnight the flaming
carriage of the very latest turns
back into a pumpkin, expired news,
money out of circulation, wastepaper,
carcass of reports and updates,
carrion already picked clean.

CODICE A BARRE

Onoriamo l'altissimo vessillo
che sventola sul regno della cosa
l'anima crittografica del prezzo
rosa del nome e nome della rosa
mazzo di steli, fascio
di tendini e di vene
—polso
per auscultare
il battito del soldo.

Let us honor the topmost banner
fluttering over the kingdom of commodities
—the encoded soul of price,
rose of the name and name of the rose,
bundle of stems, fasces
of tendons and veins
—wrist on which to take
the pulse of money.

SANTO

Quel nome che accompagna
il giorno del giornale porta
il ricordo di un corpo straziato.
C'è sempre un vescovo, un martire o una vergine
a tingere di sangue sacro il frutto delle
rotative—non olive
ma inchiostro sotto il torchio.

That name that lies alongside
the day of the daily bears
the memory of a lacerated corpse.
There's always some bishop, martyr, or virgin
to stain with sacred blood the fruit of
the rotaries—not olives
but printer's ink under the press.

DAL NOSTRO INVIATO A:

DRESDA, PIAZZA DEL TEATRO

Non troppo a lungo,
sull'acciottolato.
La statua equestre, venga
via, raffigura il re.
Sí, il traduttore di Dante,
ora muoviamoci.
Bello il teatro, bello,
però andiamo,
perché questo è pavé contaminato
(un incidente nucleare accanto
alla cava) e noi qui siamo già
larve su lastra, lemuri,
turisti radiologici, ampolline,
vetro che soffia un soffio di elettroni.

Don't let's hang about
on the cobblestones.
The equestrian statue—keep
going—represents the king.
Yes, the Dante translator.
Now let's move on.
Lovely theater, first-rate, but
no point in dawdling,
because this paving's contaminated
(a nuclear accident
near the quarry) and here we are
already like ghosts on this X-ray plate, like ghouls,
radiological tourists, little glass vessels
blown with a breeze of electrons.

D'improvviso ho visto un colibrí, anzi
l'ho udito frullare fra i rami
di un cespuglio che stavo scostando.
Per meglio dire, ho avvertito il suo brivido,
simile a quello dei centomila volts
che sibilano sui cavi, da traliccio a traliccio,
nelle nostre campagne—uccellini di pura energia.
E questo punto puro era lo stesso
che vortica recluso
negli acceleratori di particelle,
lungo le cieche nozze di un circuito sotterraneo.
O forse il matrimonio
è la struttura che conserva la forza
affidandola a un percorso anulare,
mobile e ferma insieme
(un'aureola del sesso). Eppure nel ribrezzo
che provavo per la sua minacciosa libertà,
libertà di colpirmi,
il colibrí stava prima,
precedeva ogni forma, era la folgore
che ancora non ha scelto il suo tracciato,
era tutti i tracciati.
Potenza di insostenibile fragore
era lui la cascata che cercavo
mentre andavo spostando quei cespugli.

Un amico lontano

Suddenly I saw a hummingbird, or rather
I heard it whirring among the branches
of a bush I was rummaging through.
Or better still, I became aware of its trembling
like the hiss of a hundred thousand volts
along power lines strung from pylon to pylon
across our countryside—little birds of pure energy.
And this pure source was the same that,
hidden, whirls
in particle accelerators
along the blind wedding of an underground circuit.
Or perhaps marriage
is the structure that stores the power,
consigning it to an annular course
at the same time mobile and static
(the aureole of sex). And yet in the shock
I experienced at the threat of its freedom,
freedom to strike me, the hummingbird came first,
preceded every other form—it was the lightning flash
that has still to choose the track it burns through
and so was every possible track.
The power of an unbearable crash—
he was the cascade I'd gone in search of
as I went on rummaging through those bushes.

A faraway friend

FOTOGRAFIA

È che lo scatto recide l'ombelico
della luce. Recide, quella forbice,
il filamento lento e lungo dello
sguardo, budello
del nutrimento, separa
perché l'immagine venga
al mondo dividendosi
dalla madre.
E quella pupa d'ombra,
quel bozzolo, è la cesta
lasciata a galleggiare sulle acque
per mettere in salvo la forma.

It's that the flash cuts the umbilical cord
of the light. It cuts, that pair of scissors,
the slow long filament of the
gaze, the long intestine
that feeds us; it cuts in two
because the image
comes into the world separating itself
from its mother.
And that pupa of shadow,
that cocoon, is the basket
left to rock upon the waters
to rescue form and keep it safe.

LA POESIA

Le poesie vanno sempre rilette,
lette, rilette, lette, messe in carica;
ogni lettura compie la ricarica,
sono apparecchi per caricare senso;
e il senso vi si accumula, ronzio
di particelle in attesa,
sospiri trattenuti, ticchettii,
da dentro il cavallo di Troia.

Poems always have to be reread,
read, reread, read again, recharged;
every reading energizes them—
they're machines to recharge sense,
and meanings gather in them, a buzz
of particles that lie in wait,
withheld sighs, clicking and ticking
inside the Trojan Horse.

LA NOSTRA CITTÀ: GRAFFITI

Da dove sbuca questa lingua fetale,
con i suoi guizzanti caratteri
alfanumerici?
Chi parla l'interlingua-spray
dai muri, dai tram, dai citofoni?
Cosa cerca di dire
questa citofonata lingua
che dal basso chiama?

Where does this fetal, feral language
come from, with its shimmering
alphanumerical tags?
Who speaks this spray-on Esperanto
from walls, trams, and entry phones?
What is it telling us,
this crackly static tongue
that calls from the deep?

LA NOSTRA CITTÀ:

PAESAGGIO CON SKATE

Pur di fare suonare i monumenti
trasformano in tastiera le scalinate
traendo da ringhiere
o rampe arpeggi araldici
e glissano a lungo estenuati
esclusi, solidali
nel mélos del loro teppismo
con purezza ferita
e manierismo,
con tribale dandysmo
puberale.

OUR CITY: LANDSCAPE

WITH SKATEBOARDS

To play on monuments, to make them sound,
they turn stairways into keyboards,
from railings and ramps extracting
heraldic arpeggios
and gliding, glissando, at such length
they wear themselves out, this excluded
brotherhood of music
with their coded manners
and wounded integrity,
their tribal adolescent dandyism.

L'ANGOLO DEL BAMBINO:

NINNA NANNA DEL GOBI

Soffia il deserto sul Celeste Impero,
l'Imperatore della Cina ha freddo.

Per riscaldarlo i sudditi gli donano
una sciarpa lunghissima
di pietra.

Se quel regalo non gli servirà
ad arginare il vento della steppa,
almeno sarà un segno della Terra,
l'unico che si scorge dalla Luna.

CHILDREN'S CORNER:

LULLABY OF THE GOBI

The desert breathes on the Celestial Empire.
The Emperor of China is cold.

To warm him up again his subjects give him
an interminable scarf
of stone.

And if this gift proves useless
in stemming the cold wind off the steppes,
at least it shall be a sign of the Earth
—from the Moon its one and only sign.

L'ANGOLO DEL BAMBINO:

ASSOCIAZIONE SOSTEGNO

MALATI D'ASMA

Non avere paura del respiro,
perché dà e toglie come la marea:

lascialo andare senza trattenerlo,
non chiuderlo nel pozzo dell'apnea.

Devi essere indulgente col respiro,
come se fosse uno yo-yo invisibile:

se frusciando scompare e ti abbandona,
sempre frusciando tornerà infallibile.

CHILDREN'S CORNER: AID ASSOCIATION FOR ASTHMA SUFFERERS

Don't be afraid of breathing,
because it gives and takes like the tide:

let it go free without grabbing hold of it,
don't shut it in the dark well of apnea.

Be indulgent with breathing,
as if it were an invisible yo-yo:

if rustling it should vanish and desert you,
still rustling always it returns.

GIOCHI: SCACCHI

Il bianco muove
e vince in tre mosse.
Non sapremo mai quali.

White to play
and mate in three moves.
We never know which.

GIOCHI: REBUS

È un mondo senza tempo
e senza vento.
Tutto sta fermo
e faticosamente significa.
Enorme è la fatica del significare
in questo cantiere del senso.
Ogni parola è una massicciata
di lettere e figure.
Tutto pesa.

A world without time.
Without a breeze.
Everything is still
and exhaustingly full of meaning.
There's no end of meaning and sheer slog
in this worksite of sense.
Every word is a gravelly roadbed
of letters and figures.
Everything weighs a ton.

L'INTERVISTA

Con un Q. I. che segna 154,
l'attrice interpellata
vanta la sua iscrizione
al club dei superdotati
cerebrali. Non si contano piú
le ipotesi sull'origine della
cicatrice che reca sul collo
(esiste un sito internet
all'uopo dedicato).
Anima e corpo, guaine
istorïate e criptiche, ma dove,
dov'è la terza lingua
per afferrarti, diva,
per tramutarti, Stone,
in Stele di Rosetta?

With an IQ of 154,
the actress interviewed
boasts of belonging
to Mensa. Beyond
count are the hypotheses
on the source of that scar
she wears on her neck
(a whole Internet site
is dedicated to the burning question).
Body and soul are mere
sheathings, the stuff of
cryptic legends, but where,
where is that third language
to grasp your being, star,
to transform you, Sharon,
into Rosetta Stone?

VIGNETTE

Devi sapere che il pensiero è fumo
a fumetti
come un messaggio indiano
sulle cime,
e pneuma la parola soffiata
dalle labbra
nel vetro di Murano
della voce.

You should know that thought is smoke,
cartoon bubbles
like an Injun smoke signal
on the heights,
and that the word breathed out
from the lips is pneuma
in the blown Murano glass
flask of the voice.

Schiacciata tra finanza e cinema,
ovattata stanza di un borbottare
filologico, flessuosa fascia d'alghe
danzanti nell'acquario recensorio,
sta, attutito spazio, e, diresti, muto
ostensorio, non fosse pel sussurro
di quelle bollicine che salgono,
espulse sillabe d'ossigeno,
da un motore nascosto,
fontana del respiro,
libro-elica.

Wedged between finance and films,
padded room of a philological
stammer, wafted ribbon of seaweed
jinking in the critical aquarium,
it still holds out . . . an impinged-on space
and, you'd say, mute ostensorium,
if it weren't for the whisper
of those tiny bubbles that rise
(expelled oxygenated syllables)
from a hidden motor,
fountain of breathing,
book-propeller.

IL CONFINE

Il confine tra la mia vita e la morte altrui
passa dal divanetto di fronte alla tv,
pio litorale dove si riceve
il pane dell'orrore quotidiano.
Davanti all'ingiustizia che sublime
ci ha tratti in salvo per farci contemplare
il naufragio da terra,
essere giusti rappresenta
appena la minima moneta
di decenza da versare a noi stessi,
mendicanti di senso,
e al dio che impunemente
ci ha fatti accomodare sulla riva,
dal lato giusto del televisore.

The boundary between my life and another's death
passes through the sofa in front of the TV,
a pious shoreline where we receive
our daily bread of horror.
Faced with the sublime injustice
that has dragged us ashore to let us
contemplate the shipwreck, to be just
represents the minimum coin
of decency we can bestow on ourselves,
beggars of sense,
and on the god who with impunity
has made us comfortable on dry land,
on the right side of the screen.

ANNUNCI IMMOBILIARI

Affittasi villino sopra la ferrovia
con tavernetta adiacente
il capolinea dei bus
e salotto limitrofo al metrò.
Povere case abitate dal rumore
dove famiglie piccole e isolate
si stringono—uccelletti sopra i cavi
dell'alta tensione. L'alta
tensione del censo
e delle classi, l'alta
tensione del denaro,
quella scossa invisibile
che divide le vacche
nei campi, e voi da noi.
Non toccare la corrente che ti scivola accanto,
lasciala sospirare mentre romba
via sui tralicci
nel suo cupreo fiume
intrecciato.

Small house to rent overlooking the railway
with a basement area
next to the bus terminal
and drawing room adjoining the Metro.
Noise is at home in the houses of the poor
where small isolated families
huddle together—little birds perched on
high-tension wires, the high
tension of wealth and class,
of cash flow;
that invisible shock
which divides the cows
in the fields, and you from us.
Don't touch the current that flows beside you,
leave it to sigh between pylons,
rumbling along the power lines
in its coppery
braided stream.

MEDICINA: L'OCCHIO DI DOLLY

Et pour des visions écrasant son oeil darne

A. RIMBAUD

NOTA: fino al secolo scorso, nella Francia del Nord, il termine dialettale *darne* significava «colpito da vertigine, da abbacinamento». Usato soprattutto per gli ovini, l'aggettivo si poteva applicare anche agli uomini.

Mentre noi festeggiamo il cinquantesimo anniversario
della Dichiarazione Universale dei Diritti Umani,
proliferano pecore sintetiche.
Il nome della prima è stato «Dolly»,
dal greco «Dorotea». *Dono di Dio?*
Strappatagli, piuttosto, prototipica,
teo-repellente creatura.
Guardate come il doppio la abita
e trapela dal suo sguardo. Sta lí
come un miraggio, sosia, corpo vicario,
ombra che sembra attendere il ritorno
di qualcuno.
È il viandante smarrito
alla biforcazione della razza.

HEALTH: DOLLY'S EYE

Et pour des visions écrasant son oeil darne

ARTHUR RIMBAUD

NOTE: Up until the last century, in northern France, the dialect term *darne*
meant "afflicted by giddiness, vertigo." Used mainly for sheep, the adjective
could also be applied to people.

> As we celebrate the fiftieth anniversary
> of the Universal Declaration of Human Rights,
> synthetic sheep proliferate.
> The first one's name was Dolly,
> from the Greek Dorothea. Gift of God?
> —Ripped from him, rather: prototypical,
> god-repellent creature.
> See how the cloned one dwells within her,
> leaks through her looks. She's there
> like a mirage, a double, a vicarious body,
> a shadow expecting the return
> of someone.
> She's the woolly ambler stalled
> at a fork in the road of the breed.

FROM

DISTURBI

DEL SISTEMA

BINARIO

2006

FROM

DISRUPTIONS

OF THE BINARY

SYSTEM

2006

L'OMBRA

Domenica mattina,
mi risveglia la voce
di mia figlia che gridando
dalla cucina chiede
a suo fratello
se davvero la Bomba,
quando scoppia,
lascia l'ombra
dell'uomo sopra il muro.
(Non di «un uomo»:
«dell'uomo», dice). Lui
annuisce,
io mi giro dentro al letto.

Sunday morning
I'm woken by the voice
of my daughter, who, shouting,
asks her brother
if it's true the Bomb
when it explodes
leaves the shadow
of man on the wall.
(Not of "a man"
but "of man" she says.) He
agrees that it does.
I turn in my bed.

*Indico una determinata macchia della figura e dico: «Questo
è l'occhio della lepre o dell'anatra». Ma in questo disegno
come può qualcosa essere un* occhio? L. WITTGENSTEIN

Innocenti

*Ecco il segreto dell'anatra-lepre:
come essere colpevoli
rimanendo innocenti.*

I point to a particular spot and say: "This is the eye of the hare or the duck." But in this drawing, how can something be an eye? LUDWIG WITTGENSTEIN

Innocence

*This is the secret of the duck-hare:
to be guilty as hell while taking care
to preserve one's innocence.*

Ottica

Possibile che in tutto questo tempo
abbia fissato il disegno dell'anatra
senza vedere la lepre?
Provavo a spiegare il concetto d'inganno
in termini morali,
mentre ero vittima di un paradosso visivo.
Mi accanivo sull'Etica,
quando il problema riguardava l'Ottica.

Optical

How come all this time
I've been staring at a picture of the duck
never once seeing hide nor hair
of the hare?
I was trying to unravel the concept of deceit
in moral terms when I was merely
the dupe of a visual pun.
I'd opted for the ethical
when the problem was optical.

In realtà lo dimezzano

Esseri doppi popolano il mondo.
Sembra che lo raddoppino,
in realtà lo dimezzano.

Really They Halve It

Dual beings populate the earth.
It seems as though they double it,
though really they halve it.

La lepre arriva sempre per seconda

Secondo una legge percettiva,
nessuno può vedere anatra e lepre
insieme. O l'una o l'altra,
e l'una dopo l'altra.
Ma la realtà biografica supera quella grafica
e conosce una regola ulteriore:
come la lama nel bastone animato,
la lepre arriva sempre per seconda.

The Hare Always Comes In Second

According to a law of perception,
no one can see the duck and the hare
at once. Either one or the other;
and one after the other.
But biographical prevails over graphical reality
and asserts a further rule:
like the blade of the sword-stick,
the hare always comes in second.

Al sole del nemico

Noi maturiamo al sole dell'ingiustizia.
Al sole dell'ostilità, noi maturiamo.
Lievitiamo al calore dell'offesa,
perché l'offesa è l'alito da cui siamo sospinti
nella fornace dove deve compiersi
la panificazione della vita.
La spiga, gonfia, pesa, piega il debole stelo,
le messi piegano il capo al sole del nemico.

To the Enemy's Sun

We ripen in the sun of injustice.
In the sun of hostility, we ripen.
We're leavened by the heat of the offense,
for the offense is the breath, the force,
that conveys us into the oven
where we'll all be turned into bread.
The wheat swells, weighs, bends the weak stalk.
The golden harvest bends its head to the enemy's sun.

Guarda dall'altra parte

Domanda: e cosa accade quando
un'anatra-lepre si guarda allo specchio?
Chi vede? O meglio,
visto che appare prima l'anatra,
vedrà spuntare il suo secondo profilo?
Sarà cosciente d'essere una creatura doppia?
Purtroppo no, poiché,
grazie a un apposito commutatore neurologico,
non c'è passaggio fra le due metà:
Jekyll e Iago esistono soltanto nelle fiabe.
Questa specie di mostri disconosce
la sua parte mostruosa,
senza che possa esistere agnizione.
La crudeltà dell'anatra appartiene alla lepre,
che infatti, non a caso, guarda dall'altra parte.

Who Looks the Other Way

Question: And what happens when
a duck-hare looks into the mirror?
Who does he see? Or rather,
given that the duck is first to appear,
does he see his second profile emerging?
Is he aware of being a dual creature?
Unfortunately not. As, thanks to a
convenient neurological switch,
there's no connection between the two halves:
Jekyll and Iago only live in fables.
These kinds of monsters disown
their monstrous side
so no acknowledgment occurs.
The cruelty of the duck belongs to the hare,
who, not by chance, looks the other way.

Non c'entro!

Il senso di colpa è un fiammifero acceso
che va di mano in mano, in cerchio,
sempre più svelto.
Rapidi, rapidi, sta per finire,
e non vorrei toccasse
proprio a me che non c'entro!

I Had Nothing to Do with It!

The sense of guilt is a lit match
that moves from hand to hand, in a circle,
ever more rapidly.
Quick! Quick! It's about to go out
and it had better not end with me—
I had nothing to do with it!

Due

*Strada facendo, assentandosi da se stessi, perdono la
coscienza della propria identità* M. TERESTCHENKO

Potremmo dire allora che questo tipo d'anatra
è, in verità, posseduta dalla lepre?
Sí, ma se cosí fosse, quale fine farebbe
la responsabilità dell'individuo?
Appunto: qui di individui se ne trovano due.

Dual

*As they go on, becoming ever more distant from themselves, they lose
all consciousness of their own identities* MICHEL TERESCHENKO

Could we say then that this kind of duck
is actually possessed by the hare?
Yes, but if that were so, how could
the individual be held to account?
That's the point: in this case the individual is dual.

Su una sostanza infetta

È inutile cercare di svuotare
i palazzi imbottiti d'amianto:
meglio buttarli giú, rifarli da capo.
Come vuoi che mi spurghi dall'ira,
questa lana di vetro, pulviscolo
di materiale altamente tossico,
questo franare di pagliuzze
che mi compone, che io sono,
impagliata creatura,
pelle cucita su una massa letale,
involucro appena, pellicola
su una sostanza infetta.

About an Infected Substance

It's pointless trying to decontaminate
high-rises lagged with asbestos:
better demolish them, and start from scratch.
How am I supposed to rid myself of rage,
this glass wool, fine dust
of highly toxic stuff
I'm made of, this avalanche
of foul fibers that compose me,
a stuffed creature,
my skin sewn around a lethal mass,
the merest cladding of film
about an infected substance.

Della doppiezza

A cosa pensa il cartone animato,
quando a parlare è il suo interlocutore?
Mostra uno sguardo fisso e vuoto, da animale (*weltarm*,
il «povero-di-mondo» di cui parla il filosofo).
E a cosa pensa il tipo anatra-lepre?
Di mondi, ne possiede addirittura due.
Allora quale abita, la sua mente bicamerale?
Forse è in affitto, e qui sta la radice
della doppiezza.

Of Doubleness

What does the animated cartoon think of
when his fellow creature holds forth?
He presents a fixed empty gaze, gaze of an animal
(*weltarm*, "poor-in-world," the philosopher calls it).
And what is the duck-hare thinking of?
As for worlds, he owns two of them.
So which does he live in with his two-room mind?
Perhaps they're rented out,
and that's the root of doubleness.

Smaltimento rifiuti

Monili di materiale riciclato
(rigenerato, nel caso migliore).
Mattoni con le feci e con il fango.
Un vaso ricavato da un barattolo,
un maglione di plastica,
va bene, ma paralumi in pelle
umana, no. È questo il limite
stabilito dal gruppo.
Ninnoli fatti con calcoli renali?
Se con i propri, passi. Poesie.
Smaltimento rifiuti.

Rubbish Dump

Piles of recycled material
(or at best regenerated).
Bricks made of feces and of mud.
A cup fashioned from a tin can,
a plastic pullover,
are fine, but lampshades
made of human skin
are something else. This is the far
limit established by the group.
Trinkets made from kidney stones?
Okay if they're your own. Poetry.
The rubbish dump.

Volge il viso

Un giorno feci questo esperimento.
Provai a mettere un'anatra di fronte
alle azioni compiute dalla lepre,
e poi la tenni ferma.
Fu come inserire un chiodo nella presa:
una vampata, e se ne andò la luce.
Negava. Tentai ancora. Sempre uguale.
C'è un relais, in quei disegni,
che non consente loro alcun passaggio
da un lato all'altro della prospettiva.
Per questo certe lepri sono in grado
di fare paralumi in pelle umana,
mentre l'inconsapevole anatra
volge il viso.

He Turns His Head Away

One day I tried this experiment:
of putting the duck in front of
what the hare had committed
and holding him there.
It was like putting a nail in the socket:
a flash, then the lights go out.
He refused. I tried again. The same happened.
There's a short circuit in such designs
that bars any way through
from one to the other side of the perspective.
Because of this some hares are capable
of making lampshades of human skin
while the duck, unaware,
turns his head away.

Le tengo fuori

Voci-vespe ronzano, bzzzz,
un urticante sciame
che batte ai vetri della mia finestra:
vogliono entrare, ma le tengo fuori.

I Keep Them Out

Wasp-voices hum and buzz
in a stinging swarm
that bumps against my windowpanes:
they want in, but I keep them out.

Per seppellire i cadaveri

Alle linci del discorso si contrappongano
le seppie dell'animo B. GRACIÁN

[. . .] spalancate le porte dell'animo, tosto sbucano
le fiere da' covili del cuore G. MAZZARINO

Altro che fiere, qui c'è solo una lepre.
Ma tutto sta nel fatto che la dissimulazione
si compie inavvertita.
Mi interessano loro, i Sonnambuli del Male.
(Altra interpretazione:
le due parti del volto dormono a fasi alterne,
e l'una non immagina neppure
l'esistenza dell'altra).
L'anatra ignora la sua dolce metà,
l'altra faccia della luna psichica,
il giardinetto sul retro di casa
per seppellire i cadaveri.

For Burying the Corpses

To the lynxes of discourse are counterposed
the cuttlefish of the soul BALTASAR GRACIÁN

[. . .] No sooner are the doors of the soul opened wide than the
beasts emerge from the den of the heart GIULIO MAZZARINO

Far from the beasts, here there's only a hare.
But it all comes down to the fact
dissimulation happens unbeknownst.
They intrigue me, these Sleepwalkers of Evil.
(Another interpretation:
the two sides of the face sleep in alternate phases,
and the one doesn't even dream
of the other's existence.)
The duck is unaware of his better half,
the other side of the psychic moon,
the little garden back of the house
for burying the corpses in.

Lesioni nel cuore

Ma puoi davvero accusare la figura
d'aver volto la faccia,
d'aver cambiato viso? Perché,
se ha sempre avuto due espressioni?
L'equivoco, piuttosto, dipende da chi osserva.
Si tratta di un difetto dello sguardo
che causa lesioni nel cuore.

Heart Lesions

But can the figure really be accused
of having turned its face away,
of being two-faced? How could it,
when it's always worn two expressions?
Surely the ambiguity lies with the beholder.
We're dealing with a defect of the gaze
that causes lesions in the heart.

Dentini affilati?

Nella prima fase della convalescenza egli chiedeva spesso, soprattutto
mentre si radeva, se il volto che lo fissava fosse davvero il suo, e pur
sapendo che fisicamente non poteva trattarsi di altri, faceva sovente
delle smorfie o tirava fuori la lingua «per essere sicuro».

D. MACRAE — E. TROLLE

Forse è solo un problema di agnosia,
quando cioè il soggetto non è in grado
di riconoscere una porzione di sé.
Sembrano criminali; sono come malati
che scambiano la propria immagine
con quella di un estraneo.
Narciso rovesciato:
se l'eroe greco prende sé per un altro,
il paziente, al contrario, scorge un altro
al posto di se stesso.
Bello, il mio becco giallo,
ma a chi appartengono quei dentini affilati?

Sharp Little Teeth?

*The patient would frequently, especially when shaving, question whether
the face staring at him from the mirror was really his own, and even
though he knew it could be physically no other, on several occasions he
found himself grimacing or sticking out his tongue "just to be sure."*
DONALD MACRAE AND ELLI TROLLE

Perhaps it's only a problem of agnosia,
when, that is, the subject's not in a position
to recognize an aspect of himself.
They seem criminals, but they're like mental patients
who mistake their own image
for that of a stranger.
Narcissus reversed:
if the Greek hero took himself for another,
the patient, on the contrary, discerns the other
in place of himself.
What a lovely yellow beak I have,
but whose are those sharp little teeth?

Scalo merci della moralità

Esistono due modi per negare l'evidenza:
chiudere gli occhi oppure
distogliere lo sguardo.
Talvolta, tuttavia, si dà una terza strada:
basta che lo spettacolo venga deviato altrove.
Se l'anatra fissa tranquilla l'ingiustizia
cui prende parte, questo è perché l'immagine,
tramite la pupilla, cambia rotaia
e arriva nel cervello della lepre,
sul suo binario morto,
come a uno scalo merci della moralità.

Morality's Siding

There are two ways of denying the evidence:
to shut one's eyes or else
avert one's gaze.
Sometimes, though, a third way is provided:
it's quite sufficient that the spectacle
takes place elsewhere.
If the duck can stare serenely at the injustice
he's involved in, that's because the image,
by way of the pupil, changes track
and arrives in the hare's brain,
shunted on the dead rail
into morality's siding.

La quieta superficie?

La Parola rimbalza sull'acqua,
arriva fino a dodici saltelli.
Complimenti! Ma cosa sa del buio
sottostante, la quieta superficie?

The Calm Surface?

The Word skims the water and tots up
as many as a dozen leaps and bounces.
Hats off! But what does the calm surface
know of the dark below?

Orrore

Ecco l'errore:
immaginare che la soluzione risieda
nel mistero della verticalità,
nel cuore delle acque su cui rimbalza il sasso.
Invece non c'è nulla nel profondo,
non esiste una terza dimensione:
tutto si gioca sullo stesso piano,
anzi, nella medesima figura!
Basta solo guardarla in un modo diverso.
Flatlandia.
Io parlerei di inconscio complanare,
che nel mio caso fu un complanare orrore.

Horror

That's the error:
to imagine the solution lies
in things being mysteriously vertical,
in the heart of the water the stone skims over.
But there's nothing in the deep,
no third dimension exists:
everything's played out on the same plane,
or rather, in the selfsame figure!
You just have to look at him in a different way.
Flatland.
I'd speak of the unconscious being on the selfsame plane—
for me, the plane of horror.

L'indifferenza

Trovando appena un angolino libero nella loro coscienza

F.-R. DE CHATEAUBRIAND

Sono arrivato ad una conclusione:
il Male ha bisogno di spazio,
non si può fare tutto dentro casa.
Serve una dépendance, un alias, un sosia,
almeno un meta-me
(la mamma-mummia in *Psycho*).
Serve la lepre, la bestia da delega,
un capro espiatorio portatile
che possa tollerare il peso del reato.
È soltanto un problema di capienza:
trovare spazio per l'indifferenza.

Indifference

Hardly finding a free corner within their conscience
FRANÇOIS-RENÉ DE CHATEAUBRIAND

I've come to a conclusion:
Evil needs room.
You can't do everything at home.
You need an alter ego, an alias, a double,
at the least a meta-me—
the mummified Mummy in *Psycho*.
You need the hare, the delegate beast,
a portable scapegoat
to bear the weight of the crime.
It's just a question of cubic capacity:
of finding room for indifference.

Post scriptum

Addio alla lingua

I

Di colpo, un 6 gennaio di diversi anni fa,
conobbi la mia Nera Epifania,
quando la lepre mi balzò agli occhi
e mi rispose mentre mi rivolgevo all'anatra.
Fino ad allora avevo ciecamente
creduto nella sacra liturgia del colloquio.
Comunicare, per me, significava comunicarsi
nella comunione di una parola comune.
Quel giorno compresi lo scopo del Giano animale:
vanificare, ossia «gianificare», ogni scambio verbale.
Adesso è un mondo invaso da ultracorpi,
dove chiunque potrebbe rivelare un profilo nascosto,
parallelo,
ignoto anche a se stesso.

II

Fu un'amara Befana,
quella con cui si chiuse il mio millennio.
Invece di portare i suoi regali,
mi strappò ciò che avevo di piú caro:
il sogno di una lingua condivisa.

Postscript

Goodbye to Language

I

Suddenly, one January 6 some years ago,
I met my Black Epiphany,
when the hare leapt before my eyes
and replied while I was speaking to the duck.
Till then I'd blindly believed
in the sacred liturgy of conversation.
To communicate, for me, had meant a joint endeavor
—the communion of the common word.
That day I understood the Janus animal's intent
to sabotage, or Janify, each verbal exchange.
Now I live in a world of ultrabodies
where anyone might reveal a hidden profile,
a parallel self,
unknown even to the self itself.

II

It was a bitter *Befana*
that closed my millennium.
Instead of bearing gifts
she took away what I held most dear:
the dream of a shared language.

Creature biforcate e logo-immuni
mi sorsero davanti,
invulnerabili alla verità.
Ero entrato nell'era dell'anatra-lepre,
in una età del ferro, del silenzio.

Forked creatures, immune to the word,
loomed before me,
and were invulnerable to the truth.
I had entered the age of the duck-hare,
the era of iron, of silence.

N O T E : La Befana is an ugly old woman who brings Italian children presents
(traditionally candy for good behavior, coal for bad) on Epiphany, January 6.
Her name is thought to be derived from the Greek *epiphaneia*.

ACKNOWLEDGMENTS

I'm grateful to editors of the following reviews and newspapers, where some of these poems first appeared: *Amsterdam Review, automatic lighthouse, London Review of Books, Modern Poetry in Translation, Poetry* (U.S.), *Poetry London, Poetry Review, Qualm, Times Literary Supplement,* and *World Literature Today* (U.S.), and also to BBC Radio 3. I'd also like to thank both the Rotterdam Poetry International Festival and the London International Poetry Festival, which commissioned the translation of a number of the poems. —J.M.

Valerio Magrelli was born in Rome in 1957. Among many other awards for his poems, he has won the Mondello Prize (1980), the Viareggio (1987), The Easter-Salisburg Prize (1996), the Montale Prize (2002), the Feltrinelli Prize (2002), and the Cetona Prize (2007). A professor of French literature at the University of Pisa, then Cassino, he has also published critical works on Dadaism, on Paul Valéry and Joseph Joubert, as well as notable translations of Mallarmé, Valéry, Verlaine, Beaumarchais, Roussel, and Koltès. He is also the author of two plays and two collections of short prose pieces, *Nel condominio di carne* (2003), a poignant, often witty meditation on his own body and the ills it's heir and host to, and *La Vicevita. Treni e viaggi in treno* (2009), in which he records a series of vicarious lives spent traveling by train. His most recent publication, *Nero sonetto solubile*, is a critical study of a single sonnet by Baudelaire.

.